CLASS IN AMERICA

THE
HEALTH-CARE DIVIDE

BY DUCHESS HARRIS, JD, PHD
WITH REBECCA MORRIS

Essential Library

An Imprint of Abdo Publishing | abdopublishing.com

ABDOPUBLISHING.COM

Published by Abdo Publishing, a division of ABDO, PO Box 398166, Minneapolis, Minnesota 55439.
Copyright © 2019 by Abdo Consulting Group, Inc. International copyrights reserved in all countries.
No part of this book may be reproduced in any form without written permission from the publisher.
Essential Library™ is a trademark and logo of Abdo Publishing.

Printed in the United States of America, North Mankato, Minnesota
032018
092018

**THIS BOOK CONTAINS
RECYCLED MATERIALS**

Cover Photo: Piotr Sikora/Shutterstock Images
Interior Photos: iStockphoto, 5, 11, 16, 21; Mark Kostich/iStockphoto, 8; Joe Sohm/VisionsofAmerica/
Photodisc/Getty Images, 15; Everett Collection/Newscom, 25, 30–31, 51; Ralph Morse/The LIFE
Images Collection/Getty Images, 27; Glasshouse Images/Newscom, 36; Pictorial Press Ltd/Alamy,
39; Manuel Balce Ceneta/AP Images, 43; Monkey Business Images/iStockphoto, 45; Waiter Zeboski/
AP Images, 46; Shutterstock Images, 49, 70–71; Keith Srakocic/AP Images, 56; Stigur Már Karisson/
Heimsmyndir/iStockphoto, 59; Tetra Images/Newscom, 62; Streano/Havens Stock Connection
USA/Newscom, 66–67; J. Scott Applewhite/AP Images, 73, 81, 85; Chris Maddaloni/CQ Roll Call/AP
Images, 78; C-SPAN2/AP Images, 86; Larry French/The Tax Institute at H&R Block/AP Images, 89; Seth
Wenig/AP Images, 91; Michael Reynolds/picture-alliance/dpa/AP Images, 93; Christopher Katsarov/
The Canadian Press/AP Images, 96

Editor: Alyssa Krekelberg
Series Designer: Becky Daum

LIBRARY OF CONGRESS CONTROL NUMBER: 2017961145

PUBLISHER'S CATALOGING-IN-PUBLICATION DATA

Names: Harris, Duchess, author. | Morris, Rebecca, author.
Title: The health-care divide / by Duchess Harris and Rebecca Morris.
Description: Minneapolis, Minnesota : Abdo Publishing, 2019. | Series: Class in America
          | Includes online resources and index.
Identifiers: ISBN 9781532114090 (lib.bdg.) | ISBN 9781532153921 (ebook)
Subjects: LCSH: Health services accessibility--Juvenile literature. | Community health
          services--Cross-cultural studies--Juvenile literature. | National health services--
          Juvenile literature. | Health insurance--United States--Costs--Juvenile literature. |
          Social classes--United States--History--Juvenile literature.
Classification: DDC 301.451--dc23

CONTENTS

ONE DISEASE,
TWO STORIES

E dna Riggs, a 53-year-old mother of three, arrived at Grady Memorial Hospital in Atlanta, Georgia, with late-stage breast cancer. The cancer was so severe that her breast had fallen off, a condition known as automastectomy. The resulting wound was badly infected. Automastectomy may happen when a tumor grows so large and deep that it cuts off blood flow and kills breast tissue. Dr. Otis Brawley, the chief medical officer of the American Cancer Society, reports seeing cases of automastectomy a few times a year at Grady. This hospital cares for many low-income and impoverished patients.

Riggs had felt a lump in her breast nine years before she went to the hospital, but she did not seek treatment for a variety

The socioeconomic divide impacts whether women can get basic preventative care such as mammograms.

DEFINING POVERTY AND SOCIOECONOMIC STATUS

Defining poverty is difficult because there are many variables in tracking annual income and living expenses. The federal government determines the poverty line by multiplying the cost of a minimum food diet by three. The government then compares household annual income with that line. It makes some adjustments for the age and number of people in the household. In 2017, the poverty line was $12,060 in annual income for one individual. For a family of four in 2017, the poverty line was $24,600 in annual income.[2] The term *low-income* is also difficult to define, but it often refers to people earning less than twice the federal poverty level (FPL). *Socioeconomic status* is a term that takes into account an individual's income, education level, and work history.

of reasons. She had a low-paying job with little flexibility and few benefits. She had only a small number of sick days. If she had used them up, she could have lost her job and thus her ability to care for her family. For a while, she had insurance through her employer. However, when her employer required employees to contribute $3,000 to continue on the coverage plan, Riggs could no longer afford it.[1] The cost would mean she would not be able to provide basic necessities, such as housing and food, for her children.

Riggs had no regular doctor or any routine health care. With no connection to a trusted doctor and with a fear of the financial toll, she delayed treatment until her symptoms were dire. By the time she reached the hospital, her cancer was stage four, the most advanced stage of cancer. Brawley treated Riggs's cancer with chemotherapy, but she died 20 months later.

Brawley notes that Riggs's cancer would likely have been curable had she received treatment when she first discovered the lump in her breast.

A MIDDLE-CLASS WOMAN AND BREAST CANCER

Much has changed in the United States health-care system since Riggs's case in the 2000s. The Patient Protection and Affordable Care Act (ACA) passed in 2010 and phased into full effect over several years. The ACA is often referred to as Obamacare. The ACA's goal is to ensure that everyone in the United States has access to health insurance and health care. However, the implementation of the ACA has stirred much debate around the country. Also, deep divides in socioeconomic status and health care remain. Among those in low socioeconomic groups, health care has long been associated with fear and uncertainty, even if there

WHO PROVIDES HEALTH INSURANCE?

People in the United States may obtain health insurance coverage from three sources, depending on their circumstances: through an employer, through a government program (Medicare, Medicaid, or military coverage), or through private purchase. These sources together provided coverage to 91.2 percent of the people in the United States for part or all of 2016. But 8.8 percent of the people in the United States had no health insurance coverage at any time during the year.[3] Employer-based insurance is the most common. It provides insurance for more than one-half of the people in the United States. Government-based insurance provides coverage for more than one-third of the people in the country.[4]

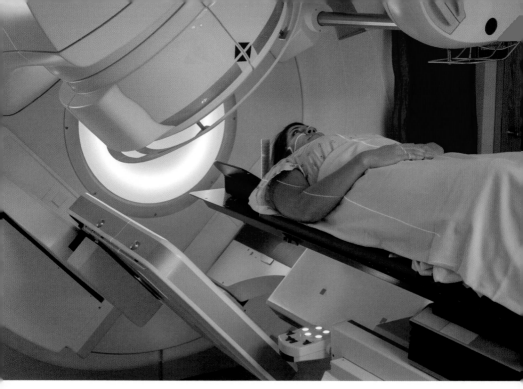

Radiation therapy is expensive. Most insurance plans will pay for the treatment.

are charitable or governmental programs available for financial assistance. Riggs had had only negative experiences with the health-care system. For her, the system involved stresses on time, uncertainty, confusion, pain, and death. The experience is often different for people in higher socioeconomic groups. Wendy Mitchell had a higher socioeconomic status than Riggs. Mitchell's story is one example of a more positive experience with the health-care system.

Mitchell, a suburban mother of three from Connecticut, started receiving mammograms to screen for breast cancer every year after she turned 40. Many health-care providers recommend routine mammograms for middle-aged and elderly women. Mitchell's health insurance covered the tests as a preventative

HEALTH INSURANCE VOCABULARY

Terms frequently used in discussions of insurance include *premium*, *co-payment*, *coinsurance*, *deductible*, and *out-of-pocket expenses*. A premium is the amount people pay every month to keep their insurance. The premium amount is the same each month. People must pay the premium regardless of whether they visit a health-care provider that month. A co-payment, or co-pay, is the fixed amount a person pays for a service. The insurance company decides the amount. For instance, a co-payment may be set at $20 to see a primary care physician, $50 to see a specialist, and $10 to fill a prescription.

Coinsurance is the amount a person has to pay for more expensive procedures, tests, and hospital care. Coinsurance is a percentage of the bill. For example, a person who has 15 percent coinsurance would pay $150 of a $1,000 medical bill. The insurance company would pay the rest. Before coinsurance applies, a person must meet the insurance deductible. A person with a $5,000 deductible would have to pay $5,000 before insurance begins to help with costs through coinsurance. After that, the person would share the cost of medical expenses with the insurer through coinsurance until the out-of-pocket maximum is met.

Out-of-pocket refers to the money a person pays from his or her private funds. Once the out-of-pocket maximum is met, insurance will pay the full bill for all medical expenses covered under the plan.

service. Mitchell's mammograms always came back normal, but then one day, she felt a lump in her breast. Because of her routine visits to the doctor, Mitchell had an established, trusted health-care provider, whom she called right away. Mitchell's doctor quickly scheduled an appointment for a biopsy. When the biopsy showed that Mitchell had a rare, aggressive, fast-growing cancer, she and her doctor established a treatment plan. The plan included surgery, radiation, chemotherapy, and regular follow-ups.

Mitchell's form of cancer often comes back, but she and her health-care providers were optimistic. Her cancer was detected early. When detected, Mitchell's cancer was still stage one. It had not yet spread to other parts of her body. Mitchell and her family had insurance. But Mitchell later noted that the costs were burdensome even for people with stable, middle-class incomes. In addition to paying an insurance deductible and co-pays, there were other costs related to care and recovery. These included the costs of second opinions and prescriptions. Frequent travel to appointments meant gas expenses and wear and tear on vehicles. There were additional costs as well, such as paying for healthy food to help her recovery. Mitchell also had to keep her house very clean, work that some people in her situation would prefer to hire out. This would decrease Mitchell's likelihood of catching another illness and developing extra complications.

UNDERSTANDING THE HEALTH-CARE DIVIDE

The differences, and the overlap, in Riggs's and Mitchell's stories demonstrate the role that economic class plays in health care. In the United States, people in the middle and upper classes often have easier access to good health care than people who are impoverished or have a low income. The inequalities in health-care access across classes contribute to what is known as the health-care divide. Illness and accidents affect people from all economic backgrounds. However, researchers often

Insurance usually pays for preventative care measures when the doctor is in the patient's health-care network.

point to economic status as one of the most significant factors in predicting a person's good health, longevity, and ability to manage illness and injury.

Researchers note that cancer affects the rich and the poor at almost equal rates. However, the types of cancer diagnosed and a patient's prognosis are connected to socioeconomic status. People in lower socioeconomic groups are more likely to get certain cancers. These cancers are connected with dangerous environmental factors, such as unhealthy diets and exposure to smoking. People in higher socioeconomic groups report different types of cancers. Some of these cancers require advanced screening technology to catch. People in higher socioeconomic groups can afford such screenings. The benefits of early screening, advanced technology, and ready access to health care were evident in Mitchell's experience. The dangers of delayed treatment and lack of screenings were evident in Riggs's experience. Overall, researchers note that "higher poverty" is associated with "higher mortality" in cancer cases.[5] Outcomes for other chronic conditions as well as temporary illnesses follow similar trends: they are often worse for people who have low incomes.

There are connections between socioeconomic status, health care, and inequalities in access to medical services. Current and historical debates have considered those

LIMITING SUGARY DRINKS IN NEW YORK CITY

Starting in 2006, New York City began efforts to reduce consumption of sugary drinks. These drinks are associated with chronic, expensive medical conditions including obesity, type 2 diabetes, and weight gain. The city approached the effort through media campaigns and new rules. Some of these actions drew controversy. For instance, the portion-cap rule was criticized for bringing too much government involvement into business and people's choices. That rule attempted to limit to 16 ounces (473 mL) the size of cups used for sugary drinks offered at food establishments such as restaurants and concession stands.[6] A court decision overturned the rule in New York. Other cities in the United States and around the world have also sought action against unhealthy foods and drinks.

connections. Government initiatives, private businesses, social movements, and charitable organizations have all worked to close the health-care gap. At the same time, there are wide-reaching and passionately held opinions about health care. For instance, citizens and lawmakers debate whether health care should be treated as a commodity for sale or as a basic human right, available to all for free. People who agree that the government should have some role in health care debate the extent of that role. For example, people debate possible government restrictions on certain health-care services, such as reproductive services, or government regulations on certain behaviors, such as drinking sugary sodas. Age, gender, and race also play roles in the complexity of health care.

DISCUSSION STARTERS

- Wendy Mitchell wrote online about her cancer experience and established a fund-raising page to help with the cost of treatment and recovery. Have you ever seen or been a part of a fund-raising effort? How did you feel about it?

- Who should decide which products are healthy and which are unhealthy? Should the government have the authority to limit or ban the use of unhealthy products?

- Do you think it's fair that people with lower incomes have a harder time receiving quality health care? Explain your answer.

TWO

HEALTH CARE AND
POVERTY

overty and poor health have a close relationship. Health Poverty Action is a nonprofit organization that studies the link between economics and health. It observes, "Poverty is both a cause and a consequence of poor health."[1] Poverty acts as a cause of poor health for many reasons. It may expose people to dangerous environmental and lifestyle conditions. It may also hurt people's chances of getting preventative care. Some people delay treatment for conditions because they are afraid of what it might cost. Poor health can lead to economic hardship for many reasons as well. Medical problems can cause people to miss work. They can even cause people who are ill or their caretakers to lose their jobs. Expensive medical bills, travel costs, medication costs, and any costs associated with changing a person's living conditions can

People living in poverty can be exposed to dangerous environmental and lifestyle conditions.

Frequent or expensive medical bills can push people into debt.

cause economic hardship. Not everyone who suffers from health problems is poor, nor will health problems inevitably cause poverty. However, there is an established link between economic and health struggles. Furthermore, medical bills are one of the leading causes of bankruptcy in the United States.

POVERTY AS A CAUSE OF POOR HEALTH

To maintain good health, a person must seek preventative care, get prompt treatment when illness or injury occurs, and live in a healthy environment. All three factors are difficult for people who live in poverty or with low incomes. Preventative health care refers to checkups, screenings, and procedures that are meant to stave off problems and detect any issues that have arisen. Many insurance providers offer plans with free or low-cost preventative care. This coverage may include tests to check for heart disease, diabetes, cancer, mental illness, oral health issues, and vision issues. It may also include vaccinations as well as educational programs on maintaining and improving health. Researchers have found that quality, personalized, preventative care can improve individuals' abilities to manage their own health and decrease medical costs later in life. Health-care experts report that in places where it is difficult to get preventative services, people face "higher death and disease rates and greater health disparities than in communities where access to primary care is better."[2]

People who can't afford insurance have trouble getting preventative health services. Even if individuals have insurance, they must have the ability and the time to travel to a health-care provider. That can be hard for people in poor or low-income households and communities.

VACCINES

Government and nonprofit organizations work to fill gaps in preventative care for the poor. One example is the federal government's Vaccines for Children program. The program provides free vaccinations to children younger than 19 who are poor, uninsured, or underinsured. The program's goal is to protect children, families, and communities from contagious diseases by making vaccinations readily available for recommended age-groups. While program participants may not have to pay for the vaccination itself, many of them still have issues finding the service and traveling to get it.

In the United States, health-care providers are spread unevenly throughout the country. There is a better ratio of health-care providers to patients in thriving suburban areas than in poor rural areas and depressed inner cities. For people struggling to afford basic necessities or people who rely on public transportation, the cost and logistics of traveling to a distant provider may delay visits. Additionally, people working low-wage jobs with unpredictable or unusual hours and few or no sick days may find it difficult to carve out time to visit providers when they are open. The same holds true for people who need to work multiple jobs.

Many of the same roadblocks also interfere with patients seeking prompt care when they are sick or injured. Patients need the information to recognize serious symptoms that require quick medical attention. They need resources to find a health-care provider, and time and transportation to visit that provider. They also need to know that they won't get an expensive bill after the visit. Delaying treatment will often make illnesses and injuries more severe and costly. Researchers have found that there is an association between delayed diagnoses and poor recovery.

A healthy environment and a healthy lifestyle go hand in hand with preventative and prompt care. The Centers for Disease Control and Prevention (CDC) notes in its National Prevention Strategy that good health stems from quality medical care as well as from environmental and lifestyle factors. These include access to nutritious food, clean air and water, nonviolent homes and communities, recreational facilities, safe outdoor space, and safe workplaces. Poor households and poor communities struggle with those factors more than economically thriving households and communities. Not all illnesses and injuries are preventable. However, healthy environments and lifestyles help stave off those that are. Moreover, if an unavoidable illness or accident occurs, a person who was healthy before is more likely to have a good outcome than someone who was less healthy.

POVERTY AS A CONSEQUENCE OF POOR HEALTH

Health problems can be costly and time consuming to manage. Even people with

FINDING HEALTHY FOODS

The term *food desert* refers to a community where residents have trouble finding healthy food options because of cost or distance. Often located in low-income urban and rural communities, areas classified as food deserts also tend to have higher incidences of chronic conditions than areas with ready access to healthy food. Conditions include obesity, diabetes, and cardiovascular disease. In food deserts, the available, affordable options tend to be prepackaged items high in sugar, salt, processed carbohydrates, and low-quality meat and dairy products. Fruits, vegetables, whole grains, and high-quality meat and dairy products are less available. In some of these communities, residents also lack information connecting diet and chronic health conditions. In addition, it is easier to prepare healthy foods in a space with kitchen appliances and tools, electricity, clean running water, and time to cook. In poor homes and communities, those resources may be limited. All of these factors combine to make sustainable changes difficult to enact and support.

LEAD EXPOSURE IN FLINT, MICHIGAN

Beginning in 2014, a controversy about high lead levels in the water supply in Flint, Michigan, emphasized the role environmental conditions play in health. Scientists found elevated lead levels after an emergency financial manager switched the city's water supply from Lake Huron to the Flint River to save money. The switch caused pipe corrosion, and lead leached into the water. Lead exposure is dangerous to all people, but it is particularly harmful for children and pregnant women. Lead poisoning hurts neurological development. This causes medical problems such as learning disabilities and behavior disorders.

In 2016, more than 40 percent of Flint's population lived in poverty. The average annual income per person from 2012 to 2016 was less than $15,000.[4] Flint also has a large minority population. Many researchers, activists, and Flint residents accused state and local government officials of racial and economic discrimination in the cause of and response to the water crisis. Flint has a long history of enforcing government policies that negatively impact poor residents and minority residents. Flint residents saw the water crisis as another example of such wide-scale discriminatory practices. They argued the decision that caused the water crisis would not have happened in an affluent, white area. And they believed that if it did, the response would have been much better. Many people believed the local government did little to fix the issue. The city increased levels of chlorine in the water to clean it and also recommended that people boil their water. After an investigation into the Flint water crisis, several officials were charged with crimes for their roles in the crisis.

medical insurance have to pay deductibles, co-payments, and coinsurance. Costs for treatment are even greater for people who have no insurance. For example, costs for a broken leg may reach $7,500. A three-day hospital stay averages approximately $30,000.[3] And cancer treatment may cost hundreds of thousands of dollars. These costs leave people vulnerable to medical debt, bankruptcy, and poverty. This is especially true if people are low income or uninsured. In a 2016 report, researchers for

People with diabetes can check their sugar levels through a blood test.

the US Census Bureau found that medical expenses pushed approximately 11 million people into poverty who otherwise would not have been there.[5]

Chronic conditions often require ongoing medication or other treatments. For instance, individuals with type 2 diabetes often need to test their blood sugar levels and take medicine, either as a pill or as an injection. They typically have direct medical costs from these medicines, injection supplies, testing supplies, blood sugar monitoring equipment, and visits to health-care providers. Individuals with type 2 diabetes commonly need to see a primary care provider. They also need to see different specialists. To manage the disease, individuals or their caretakers will also need to spend time shopping for and preparing healthy meals. They may also need recommendations for good nutrition from a dietician or diabetes educator. Fitness and weight management are also important for someone with type 2 diabetes. A person with the disease may need to consult with a trainer, fitness program, or support group.

The time and management costs of poor health combine and feed into the financial cost. Hours involved in traveling to appointments, recovering from procedures, receiving follow-ups, and managing chronic conditions may mean people

INTANGIBLE COSTS OF HEALTH PROBLEMS

Health-care professionals use different terms to describe the various costs of health care. *Direct costs* are expenses for medical services like surgeries or medical goods like medicine. *Indirect costs* are those related to lost productivity, such as missing work. In addition to direct and indirect costs of health problems, there are *intangible costs*. These are psychological and emotional costs carried by patients and caregivers that are difficult to measure. For example, intangible costs may include stress, exhaustion, anxiety, emotional pain, and fear. Such costs are hard to quantify. But over time, they can accumulate and develop into significant problems for physical health, mental health, productivity, and emotional and general well-being. For some medical conditions, such as stillbirths, researchers suggest that the intangible costs may be greater than direct and indirect costs.

miss time from school or work. This could cause a student to be less productive. It could also hurt a person's income or lead to job loss. Family and friends may also need to invest time as they help care for loved ones. If a person doesn't get treatment, he or she could miss more work or school because of the illness. Missed time at school and work because of medical conditions can have negative effects on a person's socioeconomic status.

Poverty and poor health have a close and complex relationship. Each may operate as both a cause and an effect of the other. Poverty may cause poor health, and poor health may cause poverty. However, researchers widely agree that people who are poor or low income have more difficulties finding consistent, quality health care than people who are economically secure.

DISCUSSION STARTERS

- Often people consider illness at an individual level. But what effects does one person's illness have on others? How can it affect a family, community, or society?

- States have laws requiring that children get vaccinations before they can attend school or day care. Should other preventative care procedures be required for children or adults? Explain your reasoning.

- Do you think the government should help people with medical costs? Explain your answer.

THREE

NATIONAL DEBATES
IN HISTORY

The health-care divide is not a new problem in the United States. People have discussed health-care inequalities and access to health care for more than a century. In the early 1900s, people began asking for affordable, quality health care for vulnerable and marginalized groups. This caused many people to debate health care's accessibility gap. Among the vulnerable and marginalized groups seeking access to decent health care were low-wage workers, women, and veterans. These groups saw some success for their efforts. However, the most ambitious reforms, such as national health insurance, never passed into law. Many of the issues raised by reformers at the time continue to receive attention in today's health-care debates.

Johns Hopkins University School of Medicine opened in 1893. It was one of the first US medical schools to allow women to enter.

HEALTH CARE IN THE 1800s AND EARLY 1900s

In the United States, people were not familiar with health insurance throughout the 1800s and the early 1900s. Today, there are large networks of general care practitioners, specialists, hospitals, and various insurance providers. In the 1800s and early 1900s, health care for white middle- and upper-class people usually involved receiving treatment at home. The treatment was often given to patients by female family members or caretakers, with the help of a physician when necessary.

Medical care options for the poor and for nonwhite communities were different from the home care that well-off white people received. For example, black enslaved people received care only if slaveholders determined that they could have it. In those cases, health care was provided by white physicians or in slave hospitals. After slavery was abolished in 1865, segregated hospitals began to appear to serve black populations.

In the late 1800s and early 1900s, hospitals for both blacks and whites were often publicly funded or charitable facilities used by the poor. Those hospitals were considered to be dangerous places where disease and infection spread. People who could afford to avoid them did. Similarly, American Indians had poor, government-administered health-care facilities in the late 1800s.

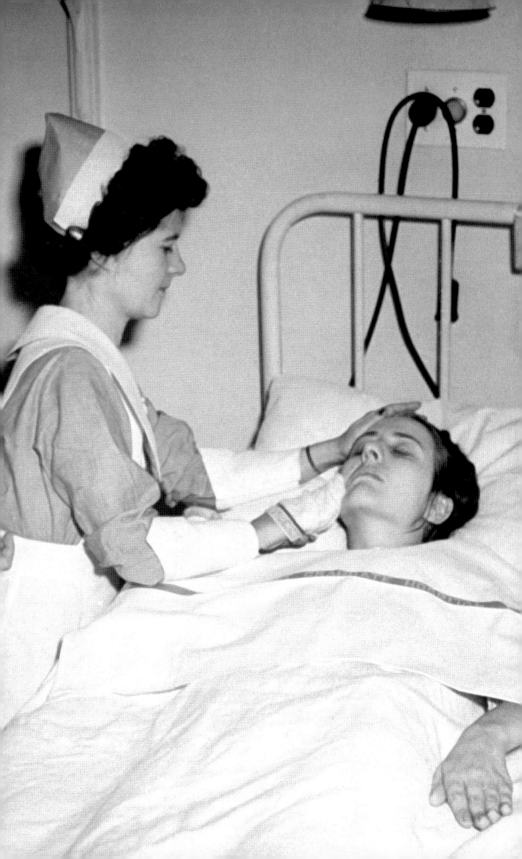

Scientific advancements in medicine, along with social movements in the early 1900s, changed the way people viewed health care. Developments in antibiotics, vaccinations, nutrition, and public sanitation helped to contain the spread of disease in communities. These developments began shifting people's views of diseases. People saw diseases as conditions to be prevented and cured rather than managed only after being contracted. Furthermore, innovations in medical technology gave doctors more specialized, advanced, and expensive equipment, such as X-ray machines. That equipment needed to be housed in hospitals and offices rather than moved from place to place on house calls. Also, cars gave more people the ability to travel to facilities with this new equipment.

Advancements in knowledge and technology caused people to develop new attitudes toward personal medical care and their ability to access it. In the early decades of the 1900s, hospitals were no longer just facilities of charitable care for the poor. They had become facilities where the middle class went for ordinary procedures. Wealthier patients began paying hospitals for high-quality health care. As hospitals took a central place in their communities, they exposed inequalities in those communities. Throughout the early decades of the 1900s, social movements exposed some of those inequalities. The movements also worked to correct them, though success was limited at times.

LOW-WAGE WORKERS, WOMEN, AND VETERANS CALL FOR CHANGE

Illness and injury worsened poverty among low-wage workers in the early 1900s. Loss of pay from missed work had devastating consequences for people who didn't have savings or job security. Making the situation more complex was the fact that people working low-wage jobs often faced dangerous health conditions. The problems of workplace hazards, poor health, job loss, and poverty among the working class were common. Reformers during the Progressive Era (1890–1920) launched the first widespread campaign for required health insurance, which they called sick pay, to address

WORKING CONDITIONS AND EMPLOYEE HEALTH

Many industries in the early 1900s used hazardous chemicals. Employees encountered the toxins daily, touching them or breathing them in. Mercury poisoning caused spasms and mental illness in some employees. The most common issue was lead poisoning. This harmed many areas of the body, including the digestive and nervous systems. Alice Hamilton was a pioneering figure in the study of occupational disease and industrial medicine. A woman in a male-dominated science field, Hamilton first took interest in industrial medicine after living and working in a social home. There, she treated many immigrants suffering from diseases linked to their work environments. Hamilton became a leading expert in lead poisoning. She was also the first woman on the faculty at Harvard Medical School. Hamilton produced several reports for the federal government about work-related illness and death. The reports helped create influential new laws in industrial safety. Hamilton's work emphasized the cycle of poor working conditions, poor wages, and poor health.

In 1909, New York City garment workers went on strike for better wages.

workplace issues. Throughout the 1910s, reformers of the American Association for Labor Legislation (AALL) led the advocacy for a sick pay program. This program was funded by contributions from employers, taxes, and workers. When individuals died on the job, people asked that the program provide financial assistance for funerals. Supporters of the program argued that it would safeguard individuals from poverty. They noted that it would also benefit society in general by decreasing the impact of serious illness on families and communities.

However, those efforts ultimately failed to pass mandatory sick pay laws. Labor activists were divided on the issue. AALL supporters wanted to protect workers through national health insurance. Meanwhile, other labor groups, such as the American Federation of Labor, led by Samuel

Gompers, wanted to protect workers through more localized unions rather than national laws. In addition, organizations for medical professionals advocated against certain reforms. They worried about losing money and their independence if health care fell under central, national influence. Also, some business leaders and insurance companies worried about the costs and consequences of national health insurance programs such as sick pay. Across the country, citizens, lawmakers, and members of various groups criticized the concept of national health insurance as socialist or communist.

SOCIALISM, COMMUNISM, AND HEALTH CARE

Fears of socialism and communism spread throughout the United States in the early decades of the 1900s. *Socialism* and *communism* are terms that refer to economic and political systems. In these systems, wealth, power, goods, and services are shared among people of a country. Communism is more extreme than socialism. However, the two terms are often linked. And some people view socialism as a stepping-stone toward communism. Socialism and communism differ from capitalism. In a capitalist system, many goods and services are controlled by private businesses or individuals. Therefore, individuals can accumulate their own wealth and power. Throughout history, the United States has been a capitalist country.

Some people believe socialism and communism pose a threat to American ideals of hard work and individual achievement. Some people in the United States fear policies resembling socialist ideas, such as mandatory national health insurance. They worry those policies might snowball into wide-scale socialist movements and even a communist revolution.

Though the AALL's campaign did not produce mandatory insurance laws in the 1910s, the movement gained some support. Female workers were especially supportive because the reforms included coverage for maternity care. Suffragists saw health care as part of their broad agenda to trigger social reform, especially where the rights of women, the poor, and children were concerned. Their support helped AALL's campaign to its only political success: a majority vote in the New York Senate. This was the first time a mandatory health-care bill was passed by a legislative body.

Women's advocacy in other areas was beginning to bring change. In 1918, Jeannette Rankin, a suffragist and the first woman elected to the US Congress, sponsored the legislation that would become the Sheppard-Towner Act. It passed in 1921. The act provided joint state and federal funding to help with maternal and newborn well-being among the poor. The Sheppard-Towner Act was a milestone in government attention to health-care needs.

VETERANS' HEALTH

A prominent legislator in veterans' health advocacy was Edith Nourse Rogers. She was the first woman from Massachusetts elected to the US Congress. During World War I (1914–1918), Rogers inspected field hospitals. She also volunteered at domestic veterans' hospitals with the American Red Cross. The injuries she saw drove her activism. After the death of her husband, Congressman John Jacob Rogers, in 1925, Rogers was elected to fill his seat. She served as a lawmaker for the next 35 years.[1] She took steps to protect veterans' health and finances.

But there were only limited gains for national health-care policy and poverty in the early 1900s.

Veterans and their supporters also saw some success for their efforts. In the 1900s, veteran health care often came through

VETERANS' HEALTH CARE AND ECONOMIC STABILITY

Veterans' health and anti-poverty advocacy grew during the Great Depression (1929–1939) and World War II (1939–1945), as did the government's response. In 1930, President Herbert Hoover established the Veterans Administration to streamline the government's support to veterans. In 1944, the GI Bill created a wide-reaching system to help veterans get education, homes, jobs, and economic security. Even with those measures, people continued to debate the best approaches to veterans' care. Those debates intensified in 2014 after a scandal involving the Veterans Health Administration (VHA) surfaced. Investigations into the VHA revealed medical facilities with long wait times, too little staff, and inaccurate and false record keeping. In some cases, those problems damaged patients' health and even caused people to die.

The fallout from the scandal caused people to start new discussions on ways to address the complex medical and financial challenges that veterans face. For instance, the VHA sees patients with conditions that are uncommon among nonveterans. These conditions include post-traumatic stress disorder and other mental health conditions, amputations, blindness, and traumatic brain injury. Veterans are also at greater risk than nonveterans for homelessness and other kinds of economic instability for many reasons. These reasons include struggles with substance abuse and mental health, troubles with unemployment, and a low military pay grade. The number of homeless veterans has decreased in the past few years. This is due to focused strategies such as creative communication tools, including a national call center with 24/7 phone lines and internet chats. The center connects homeless veterans or concerned friends or family with trained veterans affairs counselors who help identify local housing resources.

soldiers' homes. These were facilities that provided both housing and medical attention for veterans. Many veterans resisted the idea of moving into these homes because they would have to depend on the government. Veterans either went without care or had to accept being dependent. The Progressive Era reform atmosphere combined with a new wave of veterans from World War I (1914–1918) and increased people's calls for change. People highlighted services that would allow veterans to lead economically secure lives with access to health care. World War I veterans saw the beginnings of hospital and rehabilitation programs aimed at protecting their mental and physical well-being. They also saw programs that would help them find work and be financially independent. Nevertheless, those programs still had shortfalls. Health and anti-poverty advocacy continued for several decades and into the present.

ANTICIPATING CURRENT DEBATES

People's calls to improve health care led presidents such as Theodore Roosevelt and Harry S. Truman to speak up for national health insurance. Some interest groups resisted national insurance. For instance, doctors worried about losing their independence in their medical practices and finances. Lawmakers and citizens objected on an ideological level. They feared any policy that they believed resembled a socialist or communist idea. As a result, national insurance never went into effect.

Health care has changed since the early decades of the 1900s. Even so, topics discussed in those years are similar to those that persist today, although in different contexts. With different factions of society arguing various opinions, debates still center on the benefits of national health insurance. People also debate the drawbacks of national health insurance, workers' health rights, women's rights in health care and maternity coverage, veterans' health, and care for other economically vulnerable populations, such as the elderly, children, and minorities.

DISCUSSION STARTERS

- Why do you think many of today's health-care debates and challenges have been ongoing for more than a century?

- Do working conditions still have an impact on health today? Are there connections between people's jobs, their health, and their ability to obtain health care? Explain your answers.

MEDICARE: HEALTH, POVERTY, AND
THE ELDERLY

I n the decades leading up to the 1960s, life expectancy in the United States increased steadily. At the same time, medical treatment was becoming more expensive as high-cost technological and scientific advancements prolonged people's lives. Elderly adults found themselves caught in complex circumstances of increased medical needs, decreased income, and rising costs of health care. In the late 1950s and early 1960s, people over 65 were more likely than any other age-group to be poor. Almost one-third of the elderly lived in poverty in 1965.[1] To address these problems, Congress passed laws such as the Hill-Burton Act in 1946 and the Kerr-Mills Act in 1960. The Hill-Burton Act funded renovations and updates in medical facilities that provided care for poor patients. The Kerr-Mills

President Lyndon B. Johnson established Medicare on July 30, 1965.

Act provided grants to states to care for the poor elderly. But those grants varied depending on the state, and some patients encountered obstacles and inconsistent care. Even with such laws in place, persistent poverty rates led people to push for a more universal option for the elderly.

When President Lyndon B. Johnson took office in 1963, he launched a series of initiatives in his War on Poverty. These initiatives addressed a wide range of social inequalities in the country. Among these were the needs of the elderly. In 1965, Johnson's administration established Medicare. This is a government entitlement program that provides affordable health-care options to people over the age of 65. Today, Medicare helps millions of people get health care. It is the biggest purchaser of health care in the United States. At the time it was enacted, Medicare was the closest the country had come to mandatory national health

MEDICARE'S PARTS

When Medicare first passed, it had three components. This led to what is known as the three-layer-cake structure. The first part, known as Part A, offered hospital insurance. The second part, known as Part B, insured visits to the doctor's office. The third part extended benefits for the poor. The third part would later be called Medicaid, which has undergone its own expansions since 1965. Currently, Medicare has four parts. Part A still insures hospital care, and Part B insures doctor's office visits. Part C is called Medicare Advantage. It allows older adults to choose a private insurance company to administer their Medicare benefits. These plans may offer additional coverage not usually provided by Medicare, such as vision or hearing care. These plans typically have additional costs for that coverage. Part D offers insurance options to help cover the cost of prescription medications.

insurance. As a result, it was a topic of debate for many people. More than 50 years later, Medicare's significance and its future continue to be sources of political debate.

INSURANCE PROBLEMS AMONG THE ELDERLY

By the mid-1900s, middle-class adults typically obtained insurance through their employers or through private purchase. However, senior citizens who were not working found it difficult to find private health insurance companies willing to offer them coverage. Private insurance companies knew how expensive it was to insure elderly adults. That's because the elderly are much more likely to need expensive medical care than younger adults. Insurers could drop older patients or neglect to offer plans that covered expensive procedures such as surgery and outpatient care. By the late 1950s and early 1960s, reports from older people showed that they were twice as likely to have chronic illnesses and need longer hospital stays than younger people. However, only approximately one-half of older Americans had health insurance.[2]

Senior citizens without insurance had to skip medical care or make difficult financial choices. The expense of a serious illness or injury could easily exhaust any savings or family support an elderly person had. Then senior citizens would need to find limited sources of charity or welfare and hope to be approved for assistance. Oftentimes, government or charity assistance applied

THE RISE OF PRIVATE AND EMPLOYER-BASED INSURANCE

Efforts in the 1910s and 1920s to establish national insurance or mandatory employer-based insurance were unsuccessful. Private insurance companies that offered plans for individuals were still rare. As health care improved and hospital usage became more common among people in various economic classes, more insurance options became available. Among the first was a plan offered by Blue Cross Blue Shield (BCBS). BCBS originated to assist Texas teachers after Baylor University's hospital noticed that teachers often could not afford their medical bills. As a solution, the hospital established a system for more than 1,000 area teachers. Each teacher would pay $6 per year to insure 21 days of hospital care.[3] In the 1930s and 1940s, other labor groups and medical providers adapted that model and expanded it to include doctor visits as well. By the 1960s, approximately 70 percent of people in the United States had private insurance either through an employer or purchased individually.[4]

only to the elderly who could prove they were living in poverty. That requirement meant people had to exhaust their financial resources and fall into poverty before aid would become available. This system produced cycles of hardship and reliance on government support for many older adults.

INTRODUCING MEDICARE

To address the problem of poverty and health-care needs among the elderly, Medicare introduced a health insurance program specifically for that age-group. Initially, the program focused on hospital care. This was an area of particular need because it is one of the most expensive types of medical care. Since the mid-1960s, Medicare has provided a hospital insurance plan. This plan

In 2017, political leaders such as Representative Nancy Pelosi spoke about the importance of Medicare funding.

covers hospital stays, home health-care visits, and follow-up outpatient care for older adults. The 1965 law also established a supplementary medical insurance (SMI) plan to cover routine doctor's visits and other medical services not provided by the hospital insurance plan. In 1965, the SMI plan cost approximately $3 per month.[5] This gave the elderly an affordable option when other insurance companies dropped them or refused to offer coverage because of age. More than 19 million older adults signed up for Medicare the first year it took effect.[6]

Medicare extended its coverage through the 1970s and 1980s. Over several decades, lawmakers added provisions to waive premiums or offer subsidies for people below certain income levels. Various changes also took place to adjust payment structures between the government and providers. In the 2000s, new prescription drug benefits and preventative care benefits were added to Medicare. The prescription drug benefit helped 39 million people pay for their medications in its first year, 2006.[7] Preventative care and prescription drug benefits expanded further in the 2010s after the passage of the ACA.

MEDICARE'S FIRST RECIPIENT

President Harry S. Truman introduced the concept of universal health care to protect people of all ages and income levels 20 years before Medicare took effect. However, Truman's proposal faced opposition from medical professionals and political opponents. When Medicare passed years later, President Johnson officially signed it into law at the Harry S. Truman Presidential Library and Museum. Signing the bill there was a symbol of Truman's efforts in health care on behalf of vulnerable populations. At the signing, Truman, who was in his eighties by that time, received the first Medicare card ever issued.

As of 2016, more than 93 percent of adults over the age of 65 had health insurance through a government plan.[8] The majority of these were Medicare plans. Currently, Medicare's funding comes from people's payroll taxes, from taxes on income, and from premiums that recipients pay. Those premiums are linked to the recipient's income. There are also deductibles and co-pays for some services. However, additional assistance is available for elderly people who are poor or low income. For people over 65, Medicare does not deny coverage or drop coverage because of age or preexisting conditions. Preexisting conditions are those that a person has before starting a health insurance

Medicare covers some costs for physical therapy.

plan. Since Medicare's enactment, the elderly are no longer the group most likely to be poor. Children are now the group most likely to live in poverty.

MEDICARE'S CONTINUING QUESTIONS

People debated Medicare extensively before it became law. Supporters championed the act as a way to improve health care and decrease poverty among the elderly. Supporters also emphasized the benefits of health and economic stability for

Ronald Reagan didn't support national health care, but he did support bills such as the Kerr-Mills Act.

individuals and society. Other people opposed Medicare as a gateway to more government intervention in citizens' personal lives. In the 1960s, future president Ronald Reagan offered a now often-quoted observation. He said, "Behind [Medicare] will come other federal programs that will invade every area of freedom as we have known it in this country."[9] To address those concerns, the 1965 law stated that it would not interfere in medical practices. According to the law, health-care providers would have independence and authority in their practices, and private insurers would process claims and payments.

Debates about Medicare's scope still arise today. Some people suggest that the Medicare eligibility age should shift from 65 years to 50 years. They reason that the shift will give people affordable options earlier. This could help people prevent and manage medical conditions that would become expensive for them later. Others push this suggestion even further. They argue that Medicare is an effective system that should be used as a model for health insurance for everyone in the United States. On the other hand, some people point to the expense and bureaucracy of Medicare. Medicare is the second-largest federal program. Critics point out that the program needs major reform to control spending and become more efficient. Furthermore, even with Medicare in place, there are some older Americans who continue to struggle with poverty and health care. People continue to come up with new ideas about how to assist seniors who fall into the gaps of health care and poverty.

DISCUSSION STARTERS

- Should people have to exhaust all or most of their financial resources before government assistance for health care becomes available? Explain your answer.

- How would you feel if you had expensive medical bills with no way to pay them? Would you want the government to help you?

- Should those who are older or sicker pay more for insurance than those who are younger or healthier? Why or why not?

FIVE

CHILDREN, HEALTH CARE,
AND POVERTY

L ike the elderly, children have special health-care needs. However, children do not have the ability to get insurance through an employer. Instead, they are dependent on family, government, and social structures to ensure their access to health care. Events in the 1960s proved to be a critical starting point for poor children's health care, just as they were for elderly health care. Medicaid was created to protect children as well as other vulnerable populations. It began under the same act as Medicare. Medicaid was originally a supplemental program to fill gaps in Medicare, but the program evolved in later decades. By 2010, Medicaid served more people in the United States than Medicare. The largest group served by Medicaid was children.

Having a sick child can take an emotional and financial toll on families.

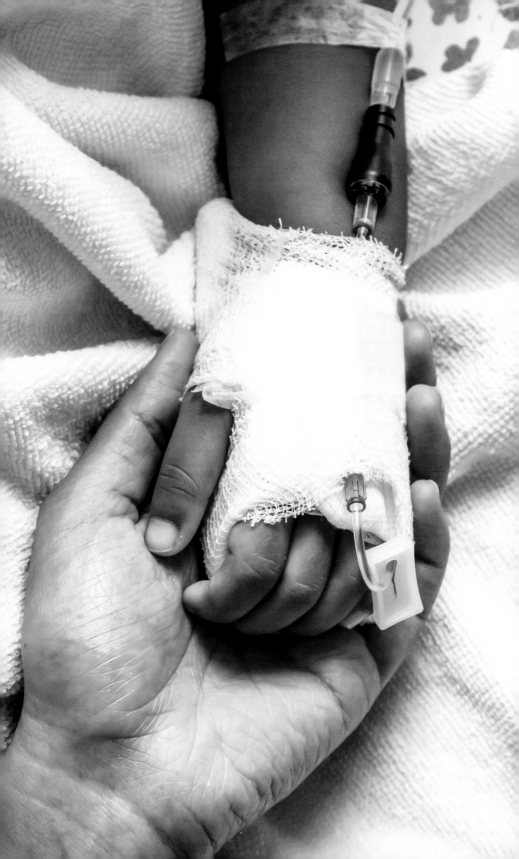

Jeannette Rankin sponsored the Sheppard-Towner Act. She served in Congress from 1917 to 1919, and again from 1941 to 1943.

Throughout the later decades of the 1900s, additional programs have developed to decrease the number of children living in poverty without access to quality medical care. Despite the work of those programs, children are the age-group most likely to be living in poverty. In addition, many of these children still lack access to regular health care. Those facts lead people to consider the impact that poor health among children may have on society. People also debate who should be responsible for children's health care.

HEALTH CARE FOR POOR CHILDREN BEFORE MEDICAID

Before Medicaid, there were some initiatives to expand federal involvement in health care, especially when that care related to children. After World War I, a study by the US Children's Bureau reported that national infant mortality rates were approximately double those of infant mortality rates in the top-ranked country, New Zealand. Many of those deaths stemmed from bad prenatal care among the poor and could be prevented. In response to the problem, Congress proposed the nation's first wide-scale health-care legislation, the Sheppard-Towner Act. Because of the act, the number of children who survived infancy increased.

In the following decades, some state and local governments established charitable health-care programs for children. These programs covered children with defects present from birth, mental disabilities, and serious chronic conditions such

CHILDHOOD HEALTH AND NATIONAL SECURITY

Regular medical care during childhood contributes to a healthy foundation for individuals. Healthy children also have broader social importance. The labor market depends on a thriving workforce. Therefore, a strong economy needs new generations of healthy individuals. The military also depends on a healthy population. In a special message to Congress about the state of national health, President Johnson highlighted the effects of children living in poverty without medical care. He noted, "Military entrance examinations reveal the consequences. Half of those rejected cannot pass the medical tests. Three-fourths of them would benefit from treatment, and earlier treatment would greatly increase recovery and decrease life-long disability."[2] Individual, economic, and military security have a basis in the healthy foundations that begin in childhood.

as epilepsy. By 1960, these programs assisted approximately 375,000 children across the nation.[1] Even so, an investigation by the Department of Health, Education and Welfare judged that hundreds of thousands of other children needed help but were not receiving it because the programs lacked funding. Also, these programs covered only severe conditions. They did not offer routine or preventative health care to poor children. As a result, many treatable conditions among poor children went undiagnosed. Children made up the largest group of welfare recipients in the early 1960s. However, the medical help available for these children was reserved for a limited pool of extreme cases among the most poor. And despite the importance of a healthy childhood as the foundation for a healthy adulthood, millions of children lacked regular medical care.

MEDICAID AND OTHER INITIATIVES

As lawmakers considered passing Medicare to assist the elderly with medical costs, there were efforts to meet the medical needs of other vulnerable groups. Those groups included poor senior citizens who could not afford the deductibles and premiums of Medicare, blind and disabled Americans under the age of 65, and poor children and their families. As a result, the law established Medicaid. At first, people didn't pay as much attention to Medicaid as they did to Medicare. However, during the next few decades it developed into a larger program than Medicare through several expansions, many focused on children's needs.

For example, in 1989, Medicaid raised the income threshold for assistance. The change required states to offer services to pregnant women and children under the age of 6 who lived at 133 percent of the federal poverty level (FPL). Living at 133 percent of the FPL means that a household earns 33 percent more money than the amount the government sets to determine poverty. Before 1989, states had to offer assistance to pregnant women and infants who earned only 100 percent or less of the FPL.[3] In 1990, Medicaid expanded coverage options for children ages 6 to 18. The passage of the ACA in 2010 expanded the program again. In 2014, Medicaid served more than 80 million people. Nearly 35 million of these people were children.[4]

They made up the largest group of people receiving medical assistance from the program.

In addition to Medicaid expansions, other initiatives broadened children's health services and promoted healthy lifestyles through nutrition, prevention, and education. Among these were programs such as the Child Nutrition Act; the Special Supplemental Nutrition Program for Women, Infants, and Children (WIC); and the Children's Health Insurance Program (CHIP). The Child Nutrition Act of 1966 highlighted the relationship between nutritious food and children's ability to develop and learn. The act was based on nutritional research. It called for an extension of a special milk program and a new breakfast program, especially for schools with a large population of students from poor areas. The breakfast program built on the efforts of the National School Lunch Act, passed in 1946. This act helped schools provide healthy meals to children who needed economic assistance. WIC began in 1972. It addressed the nutritional needs of children before they reached school by offering nutrition assistance to poor and nutritionally at-risk infants, children younger than five years, and their mothers. Meanwhile, CHIP began in 1997 to expand health-care insurance coverage to children in households that earned too much to qualify for Medicaid but not enough to be able to afford private insurance. These programs and others have continued working to fill

CHILDREN'S HEALTH CHARITIES

There are many nonprofit organizations that work to extend health care to poor children. Shriners Hospitals are among the largest and most well-known private institutions offering medical services that help close the poverty gap. The first facility opened in 1922 and was called Shriners Hospital for Crippled Children. Since then, the system has grown into a network of more than 20 hospitals.[5] The hospitals work with children's families to meet financial needs and often provide free care. There are also many other nonprofit medical facilities and wellness programs to help fill the gaps for children who face financial hardship. Some of these include Boys and Girls Clubs of America, the Children's Defense Fund, the March of Dimes, and Ronald McDonald House Charities.

Abigail Gabriel, *front*, receives insurance coverage under Medicaid.

the needs in children's health through both medical care and lifestyle factors.

THE MANY LAYERS OF CHILDREN'S HEALTH AND POVERTY

Before Medicaid's passage, children were the age-group most likely to receive welfare. Currently, children are still the age-group most likely to live in poverty and to receive welfare even though Medicaid has expanded their access to health care. A range of other programs also exist to help with poor children's health needs. The various programs show that health care and poverty among children is a multilayered issue. Researchers point out that health insurance and people's access to medical care have improved since the mid-1960s. However, those factors are only pieces of a larger whole when it comes to children's well-being. Studies note that social circumstances, environmental conditions, and behavioral factors account for far more deaths among children than lack of health care. Therefore, researchers and children's health advocates suggest that children's health and their economic well-being must be approached from a variety of social, educational, medical, familial, and governmental angles.

FAMILY CAP LAWS

Some states have enacted family cap laws for families on welfare. Those laws decrease or completely deny additional grant benefits for families who give birth to children while receiving welfare. The laws are meant to discourage people from having children if they cannot provide for the needs of those children. These caps do not apply to specific health-care programs, such as Medicaid and CHIP. However, opponents of the caps argue that they jeopardize the health of poor children. This is because they may contribute to harmful lifestyle conditions such as food insecurity and a lack of safe, stable housing.

DISCUSSION STARTERS

- Do you know of any young people who have had medical problems? Do you think it was stressful for their families to handle the medical bills? Explain your answer.

- How do you think poverty affects children?

- Do you think eating nutritious food is important for children's development? Explain your answer.

RACE, POVERTY, AND
HEALTH CARE

The War on Poverty programs of Medicare and Medicaid focused on closing the health-care poverty gap for the elderly and for children. The programs also assist people of all ages with disabilities. The creation of these programs in the mid-1960s coincided with the passage of civil rights legislation. Title VI of the Civil Rights Act of 1964 was adopted just one year before Medicare and Medicaid. The act outlawed racial discrimination in any programs associated with the federal government. Because Medicare and Medicaid received federal funds, health-care facilities that discriminated could not treat patients under those programs. The prospect of generous federal funding encouraged an end to racial segregation in many health-care facilities, especially hospitals. After Congress passed

Many African Americans face challenges receiving quality health care.

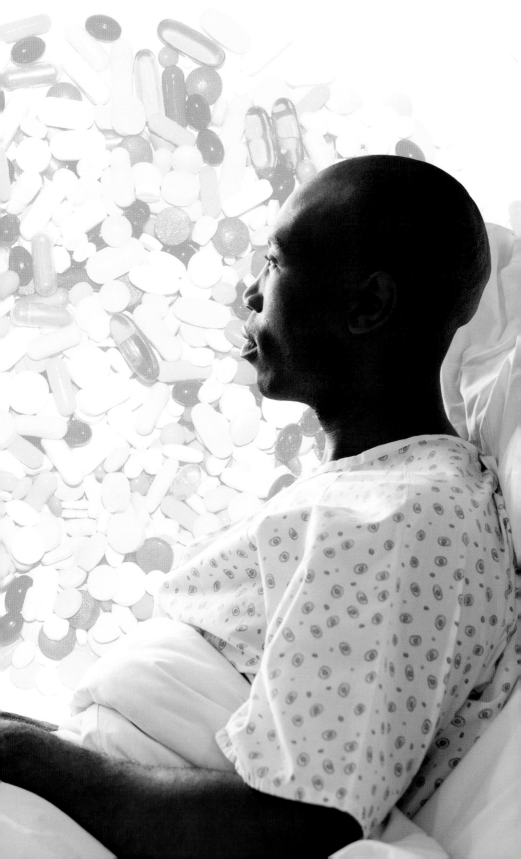

DESEGREGATING HOSPITALS

The process of desegregating hospital operations met resistance throughout the country in the 1960s. As a result, the Surgeon General's Office organized the Office of Equal Health Opportunity (OEHO). The OEHO inspected hospitals to make sure they were desegregating their operations. Many OEHO workers were civil rights activists. They took their posts seriously. To catch violations, they would organize secret meetings with sympathetic hospital workers. Sometimes, they would arrive for inspections with little advance notice. That way, hospitals could not hide segregation before the visit.

Medicare, hospitals transformed from being among the most heavily segregated institutions in the country to being among the most integrated.

Desegregation in hospitals narrowed the health-care gap in the 1960s and 1970s. Hospitals and other medical facilities eliminated second-rate waiting rooms and inpatient rooms for black patients. They also phased out substandard charity wards for poor patients. Additional separations, such as different cafeterias and race-specific blood banks, were also eliminated. Instead, medical providers used the same spaces and procedures for all patients. Rates of infant mortality and premature deaths (defined as death before age 65) among blacks declined. Also, health-care providers were spending more time and money on black patients than they had previously. Despite those gains, inequities persisted in the 1960s and 1970s. Progress since 1980 has at times slowed. Disparities in poverty rates and health care have continued in the United States for members of many racial minority groups. These groups include blacks, Hispanics, Asians, Pacific Islanders, and Native Americans and Alaska Natives.

RACIAL INEQUITIES IN HEALTH CARE

The US health-care system has a long history of neglectful, segregated, and abusive treatment within communities of color. This has contributed to disparities and mistrust of the medical system among minorities. Slavery ended and citizenship was extended to blacks after the 1860s. But these people continued to be excluded from adequate medical care.

For example, the US Public Health Service ran the Tuskegee Syphilis Study from 1932 to 1972. Hundreds of poor black men enrolled in the program. Based on information that researchers provided, the men believed they would receive treatment for their ailments. Syphilis is a sexually transmitted infection. It can also be passed from mothers to children during pregnancy. In its worst stages, syphilis may cause bone decay, heart damage, blindness, mental illness, paralysis, and death. Researchers withheld lifesaving treatment from the participants to observe and study the progression of the disease.

Today, minorities in the United States still experience higher rates of health problems and higher rates of poverty than whites. People can see health disparities as early as at birth and during

Minority children often experience different health challenges than white children.

infancy. For instance, infant and maternal mortality rates are higher among blacks than among whites. In 2014, black infant mortality rates were more than twice as high as white infant mortality rates.[1] Black maternal death rates have been higher than white maternal death rates for several decades, sometimes as much as four times higher.[2] American Indians and Alaska Natives also experience high rates of infant and maternal death.

Disparities for babies then continue into childhood. Children in minority groups are more likely to struggle with a variety of chronic conditions than their peers who are white. Black youth, especially those living in poor or low-income families, are more likely to suffer from asthma, including complications and death, than white children. In another example, research done in 2009 by the Youth Risk Surveillance System reported that Hispanic youth had higher rates of suicide attempts than youth in other racial groups. Suicide attempts in young minority children raise people's concerns that mental and emotional health-care needs are unmet for this group. High rates of depression and a lack of mental health care are also prevalent among Asian youth. Obesity and medical conditions associated with it impact American Indian children at unusually high rates. Approximately 40 to 50 percent of American Indian children are classified as overweight or obese by the time they are ten years old.[3] Obesity also affects children in many other minority groups, as do diabetes, blood pressure problems, and dental disease.

THE COMPLEX TOLL OF ASTHMA

Asthma takes a wide, complicated toll on people with the illness as well as on their families and caretakers. Researchers studied minority children who received treatment for asthma at hospitals. They found that urban minority children in the sample missed an average of seven school days per year because of complications from their condition. Their parents missed an average of six days of work per year.[4] Missing school and work worsens the effects of illness and poverty. That's because missing school and work can add educational and financial strains on top of the physical stress of a person's condition.

The inequalities continue into adulthood. For black Americans in particular, inequalities decrease their life expectancy. Though the life expectancy gap between whites and blacks has decreased during the past several decades, it still exists. In 2010, the life expectancy for black men was approximately 72 years. The life expectancy for white men was approximately 76 years. In that same year, the life expectancy for black women was approximately 78 years. The life expectancy for white women was approximately 81 years.[5] Overall, the gap in life expectancy for blacks and whites was significant in 2010. The gap stems largely from complications with heart disease, diabetes, and cancer.

Alongside disproportionate rates of health problems, many minority groups encounter disproportionate rates of poverty. For instance, in 2015, the poverty rate for whites was 9.1 percent. The poverty rate for blacks and Hispanics was more than 20 percent. The poverty rate for Asians was 11.4 percent.[6] The poverty rate for American Indians and Alaska Natives was the highest among racial groups in the United States, at 26.6 percent.[7] Rates of poverty, poor health, and poor health care are connected. Researchers describe racial inequality in poverty and health care as a harsh cycle. Poor socioeconomic circumstances foster limited health insurance coverage, poor health-care options, and bad health. In turn, poor health, poor insurance coverage, and limited care options cause more economic hardship.

GENDER AND LIFE EXPECTANCY

In addition to race, another characteristic that affects life expectancy is gender. Across many racial groups, women's life expectancies exceed men's by several years. This trend is called the male-female health survival paradox. This paradox exists in most industrialized countries around the world. Researchers suggest a combination of factors that contribute to the paradox. Among these are biological factors, such as hormonal and genetic differences between men and women. There are also factors stemming from people's social roles and lifestyles. Men are more likely than women to engage in risky behaviors. These include smoking, drinking, and violent, aggressive, or impulsive actions. Traditionally, men have also been more prone to workplace stress and dangerous work environments. Meanwhile, women's traditional roles have been more invested in active domestic work and in building emotionally supportive relationships. As modern social roles change and evolve, researchers continue to monitor their impact on the male-female health survival paradox.

People's attitudes toward health care play a role in the paradox. Women are more likely to seek preventative health care and to make use of primary care physicians than are men. Men are more likely to be hospitalized. This indicates that they wait until a health problem is severe before seeking treatment.

UNDERSTANDING RACIAL BARRIERS TO HEALTH CARE

The reasons for health-care and poverty disparities among minority populations are complex. Those disparities also have complicated effects. The severity of health-care gaps and the problems with different medical conditions vary among minority groups, especially as those groups are further subdivided. For example, within the Hispanic population, Mexican Americans may face different health and economic challenges than Puerto

Ricans. To better understand the gaps, researchers consider factors that contribute to the cycle of poverty and poor health among minority populations. These include factors at the community and national level.

At these levels, prejudice and informal segregation still exist in the United States. These have negative effects on economic progress and health. Poor minority communities are often isolated from the resources of wealthy society. In those communities, stressful and unhealthy conditions arise from deep poverty, unemployment, unstable housing, unstable utilities, high rates of crime and violence, and no social safety nets. These environments are more likely to contain dangerous pollutants that can aggravate conditions such as asthma. There may also be limited access to good educational and professional opportunities. There are often fewer recreational facilities for exercise and quality grocery stores and restaurants that support healthy lifestyles.

Another factor often considered at the national and community levels is the need for more diversity among health-care workers. Minorities remain underrepresented in the profession. For instance, in 2016, only 5 percent of dentists were Hispanic and 4 percent were black.[8] Dr. Toni Johnson-Chavis is a black woman and a medical doctor. She notes that minorities in the medical profession fill a valuable role in providing care to people of color and to people of all races living in poverty.

Not all chronic conditions are preventable even with high-quality health care. Many chronic conditions are caused or made worse by external factors. Dangerous and unhealthy external conditions often affect poor minority communities. As a result, health problems also disproportionately affect those

LOBBYING TO CLOSE THE DIVIDE

Advocacy groups have pushed for legislation to close racial disparities in poverty and health care. For example, the American Diabetes Association has led a campaign to pass the Eliminating Disparities in Diabetes Prevention, Access, and Care Act (EDDPAC) in Congress. The EDDPAC would hold the National Institutes of Health responsible for studying type 2 diabetes in minority groups, including special factors that may affect infants and pregnant women. Furthermore, the EDDPAC would task the CDC with directing culturally sensitive education and prevention initiatives for health-care providers.

communities. There are also established social and historical factors that contribute to the health-care gap. Health-care researchers have ideas on how to close poverty and health-care gaps in minority populations. They emphasize the importance of national- and community-level research and outreach. The Asian American Resource Center (AARC) is a nonprofit organization in Austin, Texas. It provides one example of an outreach program. To address the unmet health-care needs of Austin's growing Korean population, the AARC recommends holding health screenings and education sessions at the city's Korean American Cultural Center or at stores and churches frequented by members of the Korean community. Those settings would be more comfortable and familiar than medical offices.

DISCUSSION STARTERS

- Is each individual responsible for his or her health regardless of his or her background? Explain your answer.

- How do you think people feel when they don't have access to good health care? Explain your reasoning.

- Do you think it's important that people with different racial backgrounds work in the health-care industry? Explain your answer.

DOCTORS AS CIVIL RIGHTS
ACTIVISTS

A group of black doctors founded the National Medical Association (NMA) in 1895. They founded it after they were denied admission into the American Medical Association (AMA), an influential organization of medical professionals. The NMA advocated against laws and social norms that prevented black doctors from practicing in general hospitals, training in specialty programs, and seeking equal access to treatment for themselves and their families. When people debated the Medicare and Medicaid legislation, the NMA was the only national medical society that supported the bill. Because Medicare and Medicaid used federal funding, those programs could not deny patient treatment based on race. Therefore, those programs aligned with NMA's civil rights goal of eliminating discrimination. Other doctors' groups, such as the AMA, lobbied against Medicare and Medicaid in the same way that they had spoken against President Truman's health-care proposals in the late 1940s. Those groups saw the bill as a threat to their independence and to their financial freedom. They viewed it as a step toward socialized medicine. When Johnson signed Medicare and Medicaid into law, Dr. W. Montague Cobb, president of the NMA, was the only medical professional at the ceremony.

The NMA focuses on helping patients with health issues.

THE AFFORDABLE
CARE ACT

On March 23, 2010, President Barack Obama signed the ACA into law. It was the largest change to national health-care laws since the 1960s. Its passage came after more than a year of debate in Congress. The ACA takes several steps to eliminate the link between poverty and health care. First, it provides health insurance options to millions of people who lacked access to affordable coverage. This includes people denied coverage because of preexisting conditions. Before the ACA, insurers would sometimes deny coverage to people with preexisting conditions. That's because people with preexisting conditions could have expensive medical bills. Second, the ACA includes measures to promote healthier lifestyles and regular checkups. These measures help to save individuals and the

President Barack Obama signed the ACA in the White House's East Room.

REFORMS BETWEEN MEDICARE AND MEDICAID AND THE ACA

There were health-care reform efforts between the introduction of Medicare and Medicaid in 1965 and the ACA's passage in 2010. Efforts focused on a range of issues, including extending treatment and protection to vulnerable populations. For example, in the 1980s, a law was passed to protect people who had lost their jobs from also losing their health insurance immediately. Another law required emergency rooms to stabilize patients regardless of their ability to pay for treatment. Additional legislation broadened some aspects of Medicaid and Medicare further to protect disabled people, children, and low-income pregnant women. In the 1990s, there were new laws to assist with vaccines, mental health treatment, coverage for breast and cervical cancer, and acquired immune deficiency syndrome (AIDS) management.

health-care system from the costs of preventable conditions. Third, it encourages steps to eliminate wasteful and inefficient spending in the health-care system and therefore reduce costs. Obama described the law as "historic legislation" that "enshrined . . . the core principle that everybody should have some basic security when it comes to their health care."[1] On the other hand, opponents of the ACA declared it to be a government takeover of responsibility that should be up to individual consumers or states. Before, during, and after its passage, the act sparked debate about the extent of its benefits, its effect on poverty, and the role of government in health care.

EXPANDING HEALTH INSURANCE COVERAGE

In its effort to insure more people, the ACA issued individual and employer mandates. Those mandates required most individuals to have health insurance coverage. They also wanted all employers with more than 50 full-time workers to offer health care that is affordable and that meets the ACA criteria. If employers failed to do so, the government could charge a penalty payment to the employer.

Small businesses with 50 or fewer employees are not required to offer health-care plans. But the ACA provides tax credits and establishes special exchanges under the Small Business Health Options Program (SHOP) for those that do. The SHOP exchanges are designed to help employers compare choices to fit their needs.

A national tax bill passed in December 2017 overturned the individual mandate. However, the employer mandate was still in place at the start of 2018. Though the individual mandate has been overturned, the other ACA provisions remained in effect in 2018. This helped individuals get health insurance if they wanted to purchase it.

For individuals who may not have a good plan or any plan at all through an employer, the ACA presents different avenues of assistance depending on the circumstances. The ACA allows

EMPLOYER MANDATE AND REPRODUCTIVE RIGHTS

The ACA's employer mandate requires larger employers to offer full-time employees affordable, ACA-compliant health insurance. If employers do not comply, the federal government penalizes them. The ACA includes coverage of women's reproductive services that are approved by the FDA and recommended by the Institute of Medicine. These services include contraception, emergency contraception, sterilization procedures, and education and counseling on family planning. They do not include abortions. The services are treated as preventative care, which means insurers must offer them at no cost to the patient.

Research has indicated that control over reproductive choices gives women greater opportunity for educational, professional, and economic stability. It also helps them break cycles of poverty. On the other hand, some people oppose contraception because of their religious beliefs. Religious employers such as churches and religious schools are exempt from offering contraceptive coverage. But many other companies are not, even if people in those companies are personally opposed to contraception. Hobby Lobby, an arts-and-crafts store, was an exception to this rule because it is a closely-held firm, or a private company. It disagreed with contraception coverage and did not want to offer it to its employees. It initiated a lawsuit that reached the Supreme Court in 2014 (*Burwell v. Hobby Lobby Stores*). The court ruled in favor of Hobby Lobby, allowing the company, and others like it, to claim a religious exemption.

young adults to stay on their parents' insurance plans up to the age of 26. Before the ACA, some states permitted insurers to end coverage through parental insurance once a young adult reached the age of 19. Extensions were possible into the early twenties for students in college. For adults without parental support and for those over the age of 26, the ACA expands Medicaid eligibility to people who are poor or low income, and it offers subsidies to those with modest incomes. Prior to the ACA, Medicaid covered only certain groups of poor people. These groups included children and their parents, the elderly, and people who were blind or disabled. Donald Barr is a professor of pediatrics at Stanford University. He explains that the law extended coverage "to all poor people, redefining 'poor' as having incomes less than 138 percent of the FPL."[2] In 2018, 138 percent of the FPL for an individual was an income of $16,753.[3] Regardless of whether they had disabilities or children, people would qualify for Medicaid if they earned that amount or less.

Even for people earning more than 138 percent of the FPL, affording health insurance can be a challenge. As a result, the ACA also offers other methods to help people with modest incomes. Tax credit subsidies lower the premiums people have to pay to keep insurance. Cost-sharing reductions (CSRs) decrease deductibles and co-pays when people visit health-care providers. People earning between 138 percent and 250 percent of the FPL may qualify for a tax credit subsidy and a CSR. Those earning between 250 percent and 400 percent of the FPL qualify for just the tax credit subsidy.[4] The ACA established a marketplace exchange that people can use to compare plans and find subsidies and reductions for which they qualify.

Finally, the ACA extends insurance coverage by protecting people with preexisting conditions. Plans under the ACA also eliminate lifetime spending caps. Before the ACA, insurance

After controversy around the legality of the individual mandate, the Supreme Court ruled in 2012 that the ACA was constitutional. Many people saw this ruling as a victory for health care.

companies could charge more or deny coverage to people with chronic health conditions such as asthma, diabetes, and cancer. Insurers could also place a cap, or a maximum limit, on the amount that they would spend on an individual. The cap was a problem for people with long-term health needs that could cost millions of dollars in the course of a lifetime. For instance, one family's 20-month-old daughter went through a $1 million insurance cap in just three weeks in 2007 when she needed a heart transplant.[5] Another family quickly used up their lifetime caps when three of their boys were diagnosed with hemophilia, a rare blood condition. The cost of medication for each boy was approximately $150,000 per month in the mid-2000s.[6] After exhausting their private insurance, the family was able to get health-care assistance for the boys through Medicaid. However, they worried about options once the boys turned 18 years old and no longer qualified for Medicaid. Through these various forms of assistance, the ACA helped approximately 20 million people obtain health insurance coverage.[7]

PROMOTING WELLNESS, PREVENTION, AND EFFICIENCY

The ACA attempts to decrease the poverty gap by rethinking approaches that make health care expensive for both individuals and providers. The ACA does so by emphasizing prevention and wellness. The act requires insurers to offer recommended preventative services at no cost to patients. It also established programs

INSURANCE AND TOBACCO USE

The ACA does not permit insurance providers to charge higher premiums to people based on preexisting conditions. However, the law does allow insurance providers to charge premiums that are up to 50 percent higher for people who use tobacco products.[8] States may choose whether they will let insurers implement those higher rates. Supporters of higher rates argue that the rates offset the costs of chronic tobacco-related illnesses. Others argue that the higher rates only further marginalize vulnerable groups of people. Most smokers have low incomes and less than a high school education. The ACA requires insurers to offer incentives for treatments to help tobacco users quit. The kinds of programs offered and the cost assistance vary by state and by type of insurance. For example, one of BCBS's tobacco incentive programs pays the full cost of prescription medications and over-the-counter products that support efforts to break tobacco addiction. BCBS members are eligible for the incentive once they register as tobacco users and commit to a quitting date through the company's online wellness system.

GENDER AS A PREEXISTING CONDITION

Prior to the ACA, insurance providers could calculate policies based on gender. This practice was known as gender rating. Gender rating often resulted in higher premiums for women than for men. This is because, on average, women's health-care expenses are greater than men's in the course of their lifetimes. Women's higher life expectancies account for part of that expense. Their health-care expenses are also higher than men's during their childbearing years. The practice of gender rating has led some critics to argue that charging women more for insurance is similar to the practice of charging people with preexisting conditions more. Some see the ACA as a positive step toward decreasing disparity and eliminating a discriminatory practice in health care. Others argue that women's insurance should cost more because studies have found their health-care expenses are higher. Since 2014, the ACA has prohibited gender rating.

to identify and finance wellness strategies across the country. Those strategies emphasize the importance of nutritious foods, preventing violence, good education, employment opportunities, access to recreational facilities, and community environments that are clean, safe, and active. The strategies also support infrastructure aimed at preventing disease when possible and detecting and managing disease early on before it becomes severe. The ACA's position is that preventative care and wellness promotion will decrease costs by targeting the root causes of avoidable poor health conditions.

Furthermore, the ACA proposes reducing costs by increasing efficiency in government programs and in the health-care industry. For instance, the ACA created the Innovation Center to make Medicare, Medicaid, and CHIP more efficient, cost effective, and sustainable. The Innovation Center develops models that

Many Republican lawmakers spoke out against the ACA.

focus on decreasing expenses without sacrificing a patient's quality of care. Some of these models emphasize changing Medicare's payment system. Medicare makes payments based on the quantity of care more than on the quality of care. The payment system does not focus on coordinating episodes of care. In health care, the term *episode of care* refers to all the appointments and procedures a patient undergoes in the course of treatment for a complex condition. The models proposed by the Innovation Center offer incentives for providers to collaborate on episodes of care. For example, joint replacement surgeries such as knee or hip replacements are common among Medicare recipients. Those replacements often require treatment from various medical professionals, including a general practitioner and an orthopedic surgeon. Inpatient nursing facilities and home health-care agencies also play a role.

Lack of communication between offices can lead to complications, such as falls and infections. These complications can lead to more health-care costs. The Innovation Center models suggest creating a network among the various health-care offices. The network could then coordinate treatment and follow up with features such as a shared communication system so that the patient receives the most efficient care throughout the episode. Instead of paying each office at separate times for an individual service, Medicare would make a lump payment to the network to be split between offices for treatment of the episode. That payment system would be an incentive for the offices to work well together.

These models present a significant overhaul in the way that health-care systems work. The models are still in their experimental phases, but the long-term goal is to reduce medical costs for the nation as a whole by eliminating wasted time, work, and money from medical practices. The theory is that reduced medical costs overall will make health care more affordable for everyone.

SPARKING PERSONAL AND NATIONAL DEBATE

Before the passage of the ACA, polls found that "about 90% of Americans were fairly consistent in agreeing that the U.S. health care system should be completely rebuilt or required fundamental changes."[9] However, opinions vary on whether the ACA offers desired solutions. Support for the ACA among citizens consistently fell below 50 percent from 2010 until 2016.[10] The ACA presented the country with a broad change in attitude toward poverty and health, as well as wide-scale adjustments in the way care is organized and financed. These changes have prompted strong personal reactions and national debates. National debates persisted throughout Obama's two terms, were featured in the 2016 election campaigns, and dominated President Donald Trump's first year in office.

DISCUSSION STARTERS

- Is health care a fundamental right? Explain your answer.

- Because the ACA allows higher premiums for tobacco users, should it charge higher premiums for people who engage in other habits, activities, or behaviors that may be considered risky? Explain your reasoning.

- Have you heard about the ACA on the news, on the radio, or in conversations? What kinds of opinions have you heard expressed?

EIGHT

CURRENT DEBATES IN
HEALTH CARE

A t approximately one thirty in the morning on July 28, 2017, a dramatic scene unfolded in the US Senate. Senator John McCain, who had just returned to his job in Washington, DC, after being diagnosed with an aggressive type of brain cancer, turned his thumb down to the chamber. The gesture meant he was voting against a bill that would repeal sections of the ACA. He was one of only three Republican senators to vote against the Republican-sponsored bill.[1] Without the support of those three senators, the bill did not have enough votes to pass the Senate. The bill, formally called the Health Care Freedom Act, was nicknamed the skinny repeal. That's because it contained only pieces of larger ideas to repeal and replace the ACA.

In 2017, John McCain encouraged Democratic and Republican lawmakers to work together to improve health care.

U.S. SENATE | **BEGIN DEBATE ON HEALTH CARE LAW**
MAJORITY NEEDED
YES   NO
50   50

On July 25, 2017, the Senate took a vote to start a debate about the Republican-sponsored health-care bill.

McCain later released a statement explaining that he voted against the skinny repeal because "it offered no replacement to actually reform our health-care system and deliver affordable, quality health care to our citizens."[2] Among McCain's main concerns were high costs for the people in his state of Arizona, where premiums had risen for some since the passage of the ACA. Furthermore, health-care providers had departed the ACA's marketplace exchange because of the rising costs and uncertainty about the future. With his vote, McCain indicated that he did not support just repealing the ACA. Instead, he advocated for a replacement to correct the act's flaws. Other people have also questioned whether the ACA works effectively to reduce the poverty divide or whether there is a better option.

WHEN THE AFFORDABLE CARE ACT IS UNAFFORDABLE

Critics of the ACA note problems in affordability, accessibility, and clarity that persisted or worsened under the law. In 2016, there were still 27 million Americans without health insurance, and cost remained a significant obstacle.[3] For some, insurance expenses have risen under the ACA. High premiums may place a financial burden on individuals and families. High deductibles and co-pays mean people are still paying hundreds or thousands of dollars for certain procedures. Those amounts are unaffordable for some people, so they may refrain from getting care. One family who was considering doing that noted, "We can't afford the Affordable Care Act."[4]

Because of the individual mandate, those who didn't enroll in qualifying health-care coverage may have had to pay a tax penalty unless they qualified for an exemption. The penalty was paid when the individual filed his or her tax return. The law allowed the penalty amount to rise with inflation in future years. For some people, health insurance is too costly even with the option of a subsidy, so they chose to pay the tax penalty instead. That penalty may have been cheaper than insurance. However, the penalty was often still a financial burden to people in those circumstances.

One group of people who qualify for the tax exemption are those who fall into the Medicaid coverage gap. Once the ACA passed, it sought to expand Medicaid to all people earning below 138 percent of the FPL. If states did not follow the expansion, they would lose all funding for Medicaid programs. A Supreme Court ruling overturned that part of the law. The court ruled that states may choose to expand Medicaid programs or keep them as they were. The ruling created the Medicaid coverage gap. People earning between 100 percent and 138 percent of the FPL in states that did not expand Medicaid receive no federal assistance for health insurance. The ACA assumed that Medicaid

STATE CHOICE IN THE ACA AND HEALTH CARE

The Supreme Court case *National Federation of Independent Business v. Sebelius* considered the question of state authority versus federal authority in health laws. In the court's opinion, the Medicaid expansion changed the nature of Medicaid so that it "is no longer a program to care for the neediest among us, but rather an element of a comprehensive national plan to provide universal health insurance coverage."[5] The court ruled that the ACA could not require states to adopt the changes to Medicaid. Instead, the decision allowed states to choose whether they wanted to expand or not.

States can make choices independent of the federal government in other health-care matters as well. For instance, Massachusetts elected to establish an insurance mandate in 2006, four years before the ACA. That state mandate was used as a model for the ACA policies. In the 1970s, Hawaii became the first state to enact a wide-reaching law that required employers to offer health insurance to employees working 20 or more hours per week. States are also allowed to enforce their own laws in relation to certain medical procedures, such as abortion and assisted suicide for terminally ill patients. People opposed to too much federal involvement in health care raise concerns about the states' rights to make laws for their own residents.

would expand, so the insurance subsidies it created apply only to people earning between 138 percent and 400 percent of the FPL. As of January 2018, 18 states had chosen not to expand Medicaid.[6]

STRUGGLES WITH ACCESSIBILITY AND CLARITY

Access to health care is also a problem. The ACA depends on the voluntary participation of private businesses. This includes insurance companies and health-care providers. Private businesses that accept federal funds through Medicare, Medicaid, or subsidized insurance plans must follow the rules laid out in the ACA. However, the government cannot force private health-care providers to accept funds for Medicare or Medicaid and treat patients enrolled in those programs. The federal government also cannot force private insurers to participate in exchange plans and accept federal subsidies for those plans. In some cases, the federal funds that Medicare, Medicaid, and subsidized plans pay are lower than rates paid by private insurance companies before the ACA. As a result, private insurers and health-care providers have to make up the difference. Some health-care providers cannot afford to do that, so they decline patients with Medicare, Medicaid, or subsidized insurance plans. Similarly, some insurers struggle with the organizational changes required to participate in the ACA's exchanges, so they leave the marketplace. In such cases, patients may have few choices

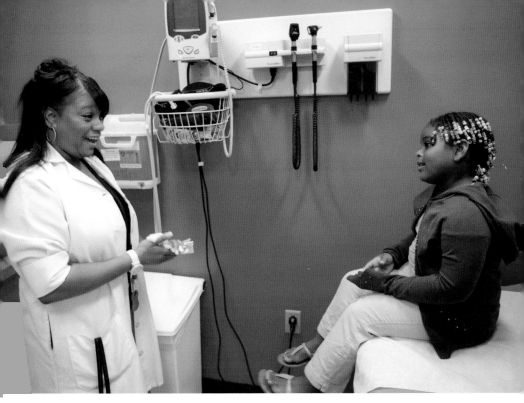

Medicaid is one of the largest insurance providers for US children.

for insurance and health-care providers. In the worst cases, patients cannot find providers in their geographic area who are accepting patients enrolled in Medicare, Medicaid, or subsidized insurance plans.

Understanding the ACA and the various paths for assistance can be challenging. Understanding coverage is called health insurance literacy. This type of literacy remains a problem because of the complexities of the law. Individuals may struggle to understand whether they qualify for Medicaid or subsidies. Even if people have coverage, the benefits may not be clear. This could cause individuals to not take advantage of no-cost services such as preventative care. If people do not take advantage of such services, it may undermine the ACA's goal of managing health proactively before conditions become severe and expensive. These problems with insurance literacy disproportionately affect people with low incomes, people with limited education, people in poor health, and people of color. As a result, access barriers persist among those groups.

REPLACEMENT EFFORTS AND CURRENT DEBATES

The skinny repeal bill was not the first effort in 2017 to overturn the ACA. Since Trump's inauguration in January 2017, Congress had discussed options to reform health-care law. It presented the American Health Care Act (AHCA) in the winter and spring after the inauguration. When both the AHCA and the skinny repeal failed to pass, Senators Lindsey Graham and Bill Cassidy introduced the Graham-Cassidy health-care bill. This bill focused on ending mandates, reforming Medicaid, and shifting more of the ACA's funding and control from the federal government to state governments. That bill also failed to pass into law. That's because the Senate did not have enough time in its schedule to complete negotiations successfully and vote. All three of these bills raised concerns about affordability, accessibility, and too much government interference in health care. The ACA opponents believe that those problems can be solved through decreased government involvement in health care. They argue that a decreased governmental role would leave room for private

President Donald Trump met with Republican lawmakers in 2017.
He encouraged them to repeal and replace the ACA.

insurers to compete. They also argue that it would allow states to make their own choices and for people to make decisions about the coverage options they want.

Wide-scale repeal and replace efforts throughout 2017 were unsuccessful. But Republican lawmakers have implemented smaller changes to encourage choices and business competition. On October 12, 2017, Trump signed an executive order to expand health insurance choice and competition. One suggested option includes looser restrictions on association plans. This option would allow small businesses to join associations that give insurance to members. Another option is health reimbursement arrangements. These are arrangements in which employers provide workers with money in order for workers to pay for health-care expenses. The ACA either prohibited or limited these options. That's because they are less regulated and less comprehensive than the ACA health-care plans. For example, the plans may not cover certain benefits such as maternity care. Supporters explain that alternate insurance plan options allow people to compare insurance companies and choose the health-care coverage they want without having to pay for the benefits they do not want. For example, if someone does not want coverage for maternity care, that person may select a plan without that benefit, which may be cheaper.

In another step to increase choice for people, Republican lawmakers also voted to end the individual mandate as part of a tax bill that passed in December 2017. This means that people who choose not to have health insurance no longer have to pay a tax penalty. Senator Lisa Murkowski of Alaska says that eliminating the mandate "restores to people the freedom to choose."[7] It also shifts choice back to state governments, which may create statewide mandates if residents want them. Opponents of the executive order and the end to the individual mandate believe that younger and healthier people will choose not to have insurance or will choose a plan that has fewer benefits. As a result, plans with more benefits for older and sicker people will become more expensive. This could hurt some people and raise health-care costs in the long run.

Changes also aim to eliminate parts of the ACA that lawmakers view as illegal. In October 2017, the Trump administration announced that it would stop federal payments for CSRs. The administration argued that these payments are not accounted for in the federal budget, so it would be unlawful to continue making them. At the same time, it is illegal for insurance companies to stop offering CSR subsidies. As a result, it is now the responsibility of insurance companies to pay for CSRs. This means that insurance companies may have to raise premiums or withdraw from offering health insurance plans under the ACA exchanges because of the cost. These possibilities have led critics to argue that the administration has misinterpreted the law. They add that these changes will undermine the ACA to the point that it will collapse. However, supporters of the administration's decision claim that this is a necessary step until there is more clarity in the law.

ACA opposition and reform efforts often focus on the belief that the federal government

PAYING FOR HEALTH CARE

In a single-payer health-care system, one entity pays for all medical expenses. That entity is usually the government, but in a single-payer system, the government does not own health-care providers. Health-care providers remain private and independent. Funding for medical care in single-payer systems typically comes from taxes. The United States does not have a universal single-payer system for all age-groups, but Medicare works as a single-payer system. Systems in which the government pays for and owns health care are called socialized health systems. In the United States, the Veterans Health Administration is a socialized system. People have debated the positives and negatives of extending a single-payer system or a socialized system to all groups in the United States.

In 2017, US senator Bernie Sanders, *center*, visited Canada to learn about the country's single-payer health-care system.

should not be too involved in health care. The ACA's critics believe that instead of broad federal government policies, private companies and local governments are better suited to meet people's needs and close health-care disparities. But some critics claim that the ACA does not go far enough in its reforms. This includes in the ways in which the government is involved in health care. These critics argue that additional reforms could help to close the health-care poverty gap.

Some people have called for a universal national health-care system. Others have supported wider governmental efforts to address the root causes underlying the cycle of poverty and poor health. The ACA took a step in this direction with the creation of the Prevention and Public Health Fund. The fund sponsors a

MENTAL HEALTH, SUBSTANCE ABUSE, AND POVERTY

In recent years, there has been an increase in opioid addiction in the United States. This has shown people how common substance abuse disorders and mental health problems are. In 2014, more than 22 million Americans over the age of 12 reported needing help with substance abuse. More than 11 million reported needing mental health treatment.[8] Researchers project that in years to come, mental illness and substance abuse disorders "will surpass all physical diseases as a major cause of disability worldwide."[9] Mental health problems and addiction can affect people of all socioeconomic backgrounds. However, as is the case with many other health conditions, there is a complex relationship between mental health and poverty and between addiction and poverty. Furthermore, mental illness, substance abuse, and chronic physical health conditions have connections. Where one of those exists, the other two are also more likely to exist.

Mental illness and substance abuse disorders take a toll on individual health and economic well-being, and they also affect larger social structures. Substance abuse alone costs institutions, businesses, health-care providers, government agencies, and community organizations in the United States an estimated $600 billion each year.[10] At the personal level, these problems may cause people to lose their jobs or leave school. The problems may also pile up on top of each other to lead to chronic unemployment, homelessness, permanent disability, poverty, and suicide.

wide range of community, care, and research initiatives. In 2017, the fund paid for a national center to prevent dangerous falls among the elderly and for a breastfeeding education program in hospitals. Other initiatives included a monitoring system to detect lead poisoning, a youth suicide prevention program, Alzheimer's outreach, and improvements to racial and ethnic approaches to community health.

HEALTH CARE IN OTHER COUNTRIES

Most industrialized countries provide universal health-care coverage, but the types of coverage vary. In Japan, all citizens must enroll in the universal health insurance system. The system provides the same benefits package to everyone, and it pays for 70 percent of medical costs. Individuals pay the remaining 30 percent.[11] However, assistance is available for needy populations. These include low-income adults and children, the elderly, and those who experience catastrophic health events. People may purchase private health insurance to supplement the universal insurance. Canada has a single-payer system that provides universal health care through general taxes. The government pays for health care, but it does not own health-care providers. Providers are private businesses. The Netherlands has a system similar to the United States' system under the ACA, but the Netherlands' system has been in place longer than the ACA. Insurance coverage in the Netherlands is mandatory, though people may choose from a range of private insurers. All insurers have to meet basic benefit standards, and there are subsidies to help low-income people. The United States spends more than other developed countries on health care. However, the United States does not provide universal health coverage, and it is not ranked as highly in health care as many countries that do.

Some researchers argue that these efforts must push further to address factors outside of the health-care system. Some factors are poor education, low-wage jobs, poor housing, restrictive family and sick leave policies, and unequal access to technology. Researchers argue that many social and environmental elements affect health. They note that disparities cannot be eliminated without addressing those elements.

Most people agree that health care in the United States needs changes because of its expense and its disparities.

The ACA ushered in significant changes to health care. It prompted renewed national interest in people's ability to access and afford health care regardless of their economic backgrounds. As policy makers presented repeal and replace options, people across the country were vocal in their support for or opposition to the ACA, new legislation, and the various ideas not yet before Congress. The heated discussions and continued repeal and replace efforts since the ACA's passage indicate that the debate is likely to persist in upcoming years. Central to those debates will be questions of efficient ways to finance health care, both nationally and personally. Debates will also explore whether health care is a right or a choice, the role of the federal government in health care, the role of the government in shaping lifestyle choices, and strategies to break long-standing cycles of poverty and poor health.

DISCUSSION QUESTIONS

- Does the ACA affect your life at all? Why do you think there are so many debates about this topic?

- How do you think people feel when they can't find a health-care provider? Explain your answer.

ESSENTIAL FACTS

SIGNIFICANT EVENTS

- On July 30, 1965, President Lyndon B. Johnson signed a law enacting Medicare and Medicaid. The law created the biggest change in health care up to that point by creating a national program to provide affordable health care to the elderly.

- On March 23, 2010, President Barack Obama signed the Patient Protection and Affordable Care Act (ACA) into law. Through mandates, the ACA moved health-care policy toward a system of universal coverage. It was the biggest change to the health-care system since the establishment of Medicare and Medicaid.

- On July 28, 2017, Republican senator John McCain delivered a dramatic "no" vote in Congress, ending a Republican-sponsored effort to repeal the ACA. The vote was a symbol of seven years' worth of frustrated efforts to overturn the ACA by lawmakers.

KEY PLAYERS

- Jeannette Rankin sponsored milestone legislation in 1918 to improve the health of women and infants.

- Harry S. Truman made the first serious political push for universal health care to protect people of all ages and all income levels in the 1940s.

- Lyndon B. Johnson signed Medicare and Medicaid into law in 1965.

- Dr. W. Montague Cobb, a civil rights activist and president of the National Medical Association, was the only medical professional to attend Johnson's signing of Medicare and Medicaid in 1965.

- Barack Obama orchestrated passage of the ACA in 2010.

- John McCain voted against Republican efforts to repeal and replace the ACA in 2017, urging instead new legislation that would offer long-term, sustainable, affordable health-care options.

IMPACT ON SOCIETY

Society depends on the health of its citizens. Preventing illness and managing conditions when they arise helps people participate in education and employment opportunities. Health care also makes up a significant portion of federal, state, and individual budgets. Efficiency in the health-care system saves funds for other purposes. In the United States, there is a health-care disparity between those who are economically stable and those who live in poverty or have low incomes. The poor are less likely to have access to quality health care and are more likely to suffer from chronic health-care conditions. Poor health creates stressful environments in families and communities. Individuals, families, and communities thus find themselves caught in cycles of poverty and poor health.

QUOTE

"Poverty is both a cause and a consequence of poor health."

—*Health Poverty Action*

GLOSSARY

BANKRUPTCY
The state of being unable to pay debts.

CAPITALISM
An economic system in which businesses are privately owned and operated for the purpose of making a profit.

CHRONIC
Continuing for a long time.

COMMUNISM
A system of government in which all property is publicly owned.

CO-PAY
A fixed, reduced cost a person pays for a particular medical service.

DEDUCTIBLE
The amount of money a person has to pay for medical expenses before his or her health insurance company begins to help pay for costs.

ENTITLEMENT PROGRAM
A program that assures specified benefits to a certain group.

FEDERAL POVERTY LEVEL
The dollar amount set by the federal government that determines the threshold for classifying a person as poor.

INDIVIDUAL MANDATE
In health-care law, a government-issued requirement that a person have health insurance.

PREEXISTING CONDITION
A health-care condition discovered before enrollment in an insurance plan.

PRENATAL
Before birth.

SOCIALISM
A political and economic theory that advocates resources and property being shared equally among members of society.

SOCIOECONOMIC
Related to both social and economic factors.

SUBSIDY
Money paid, usually by a government, to keep the price of a product or service low.

UNDERINSURED
Having inadequate health insurance for one's needs.

ADDITIONAL
RESOURCES

SELECTED BIBLIOGRAPHY

Adler, Jessica L. *Burdens of War: Creating the United States Veterans Health System*. Baltimore, MD: Johns Hopkins UP, 2017. Print.

Barr, Donald A. *Introduction to US Health Policy: The Organization, Financing, and Delivery of Health Care in America*. Baltimore, MD: Johns Hopkins UP, 2016. Print.

Engel, Jonathan. *Poor People's Medicine: Medicaid and American Charity Care Since 1965*. Durham, NC: Duke UP, 2006. Print.

FURTHER READINGS

Eboch, M. M. *Race and Economics*. Minneapolis: Abdo, 2017. Print.

Miller, Debra A., ed. *Medicare*. Detroit, MI: Greenhaven, 2013. Print.

ONLINE RESOURCES

Booklinks
NONFICTION NETWORK
FREE ONLINE NONFICTION RESOURCES

To learn more about the health-care divide in the United States, visit **abdobooklinks.com**. These links are routinely monitored and updated to provide the most current information available.

MORE INFORMATION

For more information on this subject, contact or visit the following organizations:

INSTITUTE FOR RESEARCH ON POVERTY
University of Wisconsin–Madison
1180 Observatory Drive
3412 William H. Sewell Social Sciences Building
Madison, WI 53706-1320
608-262-6358
irp.wisc.edu

The Institute for Research on Poverty is a research center at the University of Wisconsin. The institute collects information, produces studies, and suggests policies and programs to alleviate economic inequality.

THE KAISER FAMILY FOUNDATION
2400 Sandhill Road
Menlo Park, CA 94025
650-854-9400
kff.org

The Kaiser Family Foundation is a nonprofit, nonpartisan organization established to provide in-depth, factual material to educate lawmakers, the media, and the general public on health-care issues affecting the United States.

NATIONAL INSTITUTE ON MINORITY HEALTH AND HEALTH DISPARITIES
National Institutes of Health
6707 Democracy Boulevard, Suite 800
Bethesda, MD 20892-5465
301-402-1366
nimhd.nih.gov

The National Institute on Minority Health and Health Disparities is a government institute devoted to examining and addressing the health disparities encountered by minorities in the United States. The institute funds research, runs conferences, and sponsors programs in businesses and communities.

SOURCE NOTES

CHAPTER 1. ONE DISEASE, TWO STORIES

1. Otis Webb Brawley. *How We Do Harm: A Doctor Breaks Ranks about Being Sick in America*. New York: St. Martin's, 2012. Print. 10.

2. "Federal Poverty Level." *HealthCare.gov*. US Centers for Medicare & Medicaid Services, n.d. Web. 7 Feb. 2018.

3. Jessica C. Barnett and Edward R. Berchick. "Health Insurance Coverage in the United States: 2016." *United States Census Bureau*. US Department of Commerce, 12 Sept. 2017. Web. 7 Feb. 2018.

4. Barnett and Berchick, "Health Insurance Coverage in the United States: 2016."

5. Francis P. Boscoe, et al. "The Relationship Between Area Poverty and Site-Specific Cancer Incidence in the United States." *Cancer* 120:14 (2014): 2191–2198. Print.

6. Susan M. Kansagra, et al. "Reducing Sugary Drink Consumption: New York City's Approach." *American Journal of Public Health* 105.4 (2015): 61–64. Print.

CHAPTER 2. HEALTH CARE AND POVERTY

1. "Key Facts: Poverty and Poor Health." *Health Poverty Action*. Health Poverty Action, n.d. Web. 7 Feb. 2018.

2. Thomas Bodenheimer and Hoangmai H. Pham. "Primary Care: Current Problems and Proposed Solutions." *Health Affairs* 29.5 (2010). Print.

3. "Why Health Insurance Is Important." *HealthCare.gov*. US Centers for Medicare & Medicaid Services, n.d. Web. 7 Feb. 2018.

4. "Quick Facts: Flint City, Michigan." *United States Census Bureau*. US Department of Commerce, n.d. Web. 7 Feb. 2018.

5. Trudi Renwick and Liana Fox. "The Supplemental Poverty Measure: 2015." *United States Census Bureau*. US Department of Commerce, Sept. 2016. Web. 7 Feb. 2018.

CHAPTER 3. NATIONAL DEBATES IN HISTORY

1. "Rogers, Edith Nourse." *History, Art & Archives*. Office of Art & Archives, n.d. Web. 7 Feb. 2018.

CHAPTER 4. MEDICARE: HEALTH, POVERTY, AND THE ELDERLY

1. Nancy De Lew. "Medicare: 35 Years of Service." *Health Care Finance Reform* 22.1 (2000): 30–31. Print.

2. "Medicare and Medicaid: Milestones 1937–2015." *Centers for Medicare & Medicaid Services*. US Centers for Medicare & Medicaid Services, July 2015. Web. 7 Feb. 2018.

3. "Our History." *Blue Cross Blue Shield*. Blue Cross Blue Shield, n.d. Web. 7 Feb. 2018.

4. "History of Health Insurance in the United States." *American College of Healthcare Executives*. American College of Healthcare Executives, n.d. Web. 7 Feb. 2018.

5. "History of SSA During the Johnson Administration 1963–1968." *Social Security*. Social Security Administration, n.d. Web. 7 Feb. 2018.

6. "Medicare and Medicaid: Milestones 1937–2015."

7. "Medicare and Medicaid: Milestones 1937–2015."

8. Jessica C. Barnett and Edward R. Berchick. "Health Insurance Coverage in the United States: 2016." *United States Census Bureau*. US Department of Commerce, 12 Sept. 2017. Web. 7 Feb. 2018.

9. Glenn Cohen, et al, eds. *The Oxford Handbook of U.S. Health Law*. New York: Oxford UP, 2017. Print. 742–765.

CHAPTER 5. CHILDREN, HEALTH CARE, AND POVERTY

1. Jonathan Engel. *Poor People's Medicine: Medicaid and American Charity Care Since 1965*. Durham, NC: Duke UP, 2006. Print. 18.

2. Lyndon B. Johnson. "Special Message to the Congress: 'Advancing the Nation's Health.'" *American Presidency Project*. American Presidency Project, 7 Jan. 1965. Web. 7 Feb. 2018.

3. Christie Provost and Paul Hughes. "Medicaid: 35 Years of Service." *Health Care Finance Reform* 22.1 (2000): 141–174. Print.

4. "Medicaid Enrollees by Enrollment Group." *Kaiser Family Foundation*. Kaiser Family Foundation, n.d. Web. 7 Feb. 2018.

5. "About Us." *Shriners Hospital for Children—Greenville*. Shriners Hospital for Children, n.d. Web. 7 Feb. 2018.

SOURCE NOTES
CONTINUED

CHAPTER 6. RACE, POVERTY, AND HEALTH CARE

1. "Infant Mortality and African Americans." *Office of Minority Health*. US Department of Health and Human Services, n.d. Web. 7 Feb. 2018.

2. Paul Hunt and Tony Gray, eds. *Maternal Mortality, Human Rights and Accountability*. New York: Routledge, 2013. Print.

3. D. M. Styne. "Childhood Obesity in American Indians." *Journal of Public Health Management* 16.5 (2010). Print.

4. Glenn Flores, et al. "Urban Minority Children with Asthma: Substantial Morbidity, Compromised Quality and Access to Specialists, and the Importance of Poverty and Specialty Care." *Journal of Asthma* 46.4 (2009): 392–398. Print.

5. Kenneth D. Kochanek, et al. "How Did Cause of Death Contribute to Racial Differences in Life Expectancy in the United States in 2010?" *Centers for Disease Control and Prevention*. US Department of Health & Human Services, July 2013. Web. 7 Feb. 2018.

6. "Who Is Poor?" *Institute for Research on Poverty*. Board of Regents of the University of Wisconsin System, n.d. Web. 7 Feb. 2018.

7. "Facts for Features: American Indian and Alaska Native Heritage Month: November 2016." *United States Census Bureau*. US Department of Commerce, 2 Nov. 2016. Web. 7 Feb. 2018.

8. "Racial and Ethnic Diversity among Dentists in the US." *American Dental Association*. American Dental Association, n.d. Web. 7 Feb. 2018.

CHAPTER 7. THE AFFORDABLE CARE ACT

1. Barack Obama. "Remarks on Signing the Patient Protection and Affordable Care Act." *American Presidency Project*. American Presidency Project, 23 Mar. 2010. Web. 7 Feb. 2018.

2. Donald A Barr. *Introduction to US Health Policy: The Organization, Financing, and Delivery of Health Care in America*. Baltimore, MD: Johns Hopkins UP, 2016. Print. 14.

3. "Poverty Guidelines." *ASPE*. US Department of Health & Human Services, n.d. Web. 23 Mar. 2018.

4. "What's the Federal Poverty Level?" *Blue Cross Blue Shield*. Blue Cross Blue Shield, n.d. Web. 7 Feb. 2018.

5. "Health Insurance Caps Leave Patients Stranded." *NBC News*. NBCNews.com, 13 July 2008. Web. 7 Feb. 2018.

6. Christopher Lee. "More Hitting Cost Limit on Health Benefits." *Washington Post*. Washington Post Company, 27 Jan. 2008. Web. 7 Feb. 2018.

7. Stacey McMorrow and Daniel Polsky. "Insurance Coverage and Access to Care under the Affordable Care Act." *Leonard Davis Institute of Health Economics*. University of Pennsylvania, 8 Dec. 2016. Web. 7 Feb. 2018.

8. "How the Affordable Care Act Affects Tobacco Use and Control." *SAMHSA–HRSA Center for Integrated Health Solutions*. US Department of Health and Human Services, n.d. Web. 7 Feb. 2018.

9. Barr, *Introduction to US Health Policy: The Organization, Financing, and Delivery of Health Care in America*, 2.

10. Hannah Fingerhut. "Support for 2010 Health Care Law Reaches New High." *Pew Research Center*. Pew Research Center, 23 Feb. 2017. Web. 7 Feb. 2018.

CHAPTER 8. CURRENT DEBATES IN HEALTH CARE

1. Robert Pear and Thomas Kaplan. "Senate Rejects Slimmed-Down Obamacare Repeal as McCain Votes No." *New York Times*. New York Times Company, 27 July 2017. Web. 7 Feb. 2018.

2. John McCain. "Statement by Senator John McCain on Voting 'No' on 'Skinny Repeal.'" *John McCain*. US Senate, 28 July 2017. Web. 7 Feb. 2018.

3. Stacey McMorrow and Daniel Polsky. "Insurance Coverage and Access to Care under the Affordable Care Act." *Leonard Davis Institute of Health Economics*. University of Pennsylvania, 8 Dec. 2016. Web. 7 Feb. 2018.

4. Tracey Jan. "Critics Say High Deductibles Make Insurance 'Unaffordable.'" *Boston Globe*. Boston Globe Media Partners, 16 Nov. 2015. Web. 7 Feb. 2018.

5. Donald A. Barr. *Introduction to US Health Policy: The Organization, Financing, and Delivery of Health Care in America*. Baltimore, MD: Johns Hopkins UP, 2016. Print. 14.

6. "A 50-State Look at Medicaid Expansion." *Families USA*. Families USA, Jan. 2018. Web. 7 Feb. 2018.

7. Yasmeen Abutaleb. "US Senate Tax Bill Accomplishes Major Obamacare Repeal Goal." *Reuters*. Reuters, 2 Dec. 2017. Web. 7 Feb. 2018.

8. "Prevention of Substance Abuse and Mental Illness." *Substance Abuse and Mental Health Services Administration*. US Department of Health and Human Services, 20 Sept. 2017. Web. 7 Feb. 2018.

9. "Prevention of Substance Abuse and Mental Illness."

10. "Prevention of Substance Abuse and Mental Illness."

11. Ryozo Matsuda. "The Japanese Health Care System." *International Health Care System Profiles*. Commonwealth Fund, n.d. Web. 7 Feb. 2018.

INDEX

ABOUT THE
AUTHORS

DUCHESS HARRIS, JD, PHD

Professor Harris is the chair of the American Studies department at Macalester College and curator of the Duchess Harris Collection of ABDO books. She is the author and coauthor of recently released ABDO books including *Hidden Human Computers: The Black Women of NASA*, *Black Lives Matter*, and *Race and Policing*.

Before working with ABDO, she authored several other books on the topics of race, culture, and American history. She served as an associate editor for *Litigation News*, the American Bar Association Section of Litigation's quarterly flagship publication, and was the first editor in chief of *Law Raza*, an interactive online journal covering race and the law, published at William Mitchell College of Law. She has earned a PhD in American Studies from the University of Minnesota and a JD from William Mitchell College of Law.

REBECCA MORRIS

Rebecca Morris has a PhD in English from Texas A&M University. She is the author of several nonfiction books for students. Morris also writes literature guides for education websites.